The Charity
Organisation Society

C. B. P. Bosanquet

THE CHARITY

ORGANISATION SOCIETY

1869-1913

ITS IDEAS AND WORK

CHARLES LOCH MOWAT

METHUEN & CO LTD

36 Essex Street · London WC2

Printed in Great Britain by
T. & A. Constable Ltd.
Hopetoun Street, Edinburgh
Cat. No. 2/6445/10

Contents

Illustrations

Preface

The Charity Organisation Society, in its form, its work, its ideas, was a characteristic product of Victorian life and society. Apart from this, its history is the history of an idea now somewhat discredited – that of individual responsibility – and of a method now generally followed in helping families and persons in trouble – that of casework by professional social workers. It is also the history of a leader in what became an international movement. What I have attempted is no more than an introduction to its history. I have been concerned with the C.O.S., not with the history of charity or social thought in Victorian England, though I have tried to suggest the context in which the C.O.S. worked. And I have dealt chiefly with its public activities. Its domestic history would be a tale of another kind, and perhaps not one of general interest: the work of the Council and its committees, the occasional disputes and controversies, the confidential reports, the relations of Council and District Committees.

I must admit to some inherited interest in the subject, since it was my grandfather, Sir Charles Loch, who guided the C.O.S. during most of the period of its greatest influence. I have tried to avoid the extremes of partiality and of criticism, but may not have entirely succeeded. I am much indebted to Mr B. E. Astbury and Mr H. R. Durham, successively General Secretaries of the Family Welfare Association, and to the other members of the friendly staff of the Association at Denison House, for permission to use the library, first assembled by the C.O.S., and for help and advice. I gratefully acknowledge the permission of the

Preface

F.W.A. to reproduce the photograph of C. B. P. Bosanquet and the Sargent portrait of Loch. Much of the book was written while I was on the faculty of the University of Chicago, and my debt to that great university and to its fine library with its rich resources for Victorian social history is very large. My chief debt is to my mother, who by her memories of her father, her collection of his letters and her practice of his ideas of charity has inspired my interest in the C.O.S.

Bangor   C. L. M.
March, 1960

CHAPTER I

The Background of Ideas, and the Founding of the C.O.S.

When the Charity Organisation Society was founded in London in 1869 the Victorian Age, if measured by the reign of Queen Victoria, had just reached the middle of its span. The C.O.S. was a child of this middle age, of a time of contrasts – progress and pessimism, wealth and poverty, self-confidence and scepticism; it presupposed a leisured class with the means and the time to devote to charity and the 'consciousness of sin' (as Beatrice Webb has called it) to impel it to do so. In the next forty years it grew to a position of weight and influence as its ideas spread not only in Great Britain but also in the United States, the new countries of the British Empire and to some extent in continental Europe. The First World War, in which social and political changes which had already begun reached a rapid maturity, ended much of the work and influence of the C.O.S., though in smaller ways it still continues a useful life under another name.

The history of such an enterprise in the years of its strength would merit a place in the still unwritten history of Victorian charity and social work. The C.O.S. deserves, however, the individual consideration which it preached to its members and gave to those it helped, and for two special reasons: its idea and its method. The C.O.S. embodied an idea of charity which claimed to reconcile the divisions in society, to remove poverty and to produce a happy, self-reliant community. It believed that the most serious aspect of poverty was the degradation of the character of the poor man or woman. Indiscriminate charity only made things worse; it demoralised. True charity demanded friendship, thought, the sort of help that would restore a man's self-respect and his ability to support himself and his family. It asked much forbearance, no doubt, of those it helped; but it also demanded much hard work and service from the fortunate classes of the community.

The 'organisation' of charity, which began as an attempt to co-ordinate the work of charitable societies and the Poor Law, thus became a movement to reform the spirit not only of charities but of society. It offered an alternative to socialism as a means of realising a better society. It failed, as it was perhaps bound to do. But the very attempt epitomises much in Victorian life, and its influence in its heyday deserves some commemoration. And in its method the C.O.S. has left us a legacy of enduring value; for in carrying out its idea of charity the C.O.S. used and popularised the method of case-work and helped to found the profession of social worker. To the C.O.S. the method and the idea were indissolubly linked, each indispensable to the other; but in fact the method has survived in a world which has rejected much though not all of the ideals associated with it.

Charities and charitable societies abounded in Victorian Britain. Voluntary hospitals, Dr Barnardo's homes (1870), convalescent homes, the Children's Country Holiday Fund, the Metropolitan Association for Befriending Young Servants, the Y.M.C.A. (1849), the Boys' Brigade (1883), the National Institute for the Blind, the Salvation Army (1878): the list could be extended almost without end.[1] According to one estimate, the number of charities which were founded in-

---

[1] For a modern listing of charities and sketches of some of their founders see Lord Beveridge, *Voluntary Action: a Report on Methods of Social Advance* (1948).

creased every decade; 27 in 1811-20, 90 in 1861-70, 136 in 1881-90.[1] The C.O.S. was only one member of the army of the good and was unique not in its features (for instance, its emphasis on personal service) so much as in its combination of casework and an explicit social philosophy. Why did the C.O.S. come into being when it did, towards the end of the 1860's? The worst consequences of the Industrial Revolution had been mitigated; no longer could the outskirts of London and the new, raw quarters of the northern towns be called, as Chadwick had called them, 'an encamped horde, or an undisciplined soldiery'. The unrest of the 'forties, with the Chartist rallies, the propaganda of the Anti-Corn Law League, the fluctuations of employment in the early days of railway construction, was in the past. But much remained to be done to overcome the degradation and the anarchy which the rapid growth of population and industry had brought about. Dickens was still describing in his novels the poor of London, the rookeries such as 'Tom-all-Alone's' in *Bleak House* where so many families lived, crammed together in damp, verminous rooms where the light of day seldom penetrated and rats might attack a sleeping baby. Much of London was still a maze of courts and lanes and alleys where no decent person would go and the police would venture only in pairs. Henry Mayhew's four volumes on *London Labour and the London Poor* were published in 1861-62 and described, on the basis of Mayhew's conversations on his endless wanderings through the streets, not only the underworld of prostitutes, thieves, swindlers and beggars – 'those that will not work' – but also the ranks of the industrious: the street-sellers, match girls, 'Hindu tract

[1] Una Cormack, 'Developments in Case-work', in *Voluntary Social Services: Their Place in the Modern State* (1945), ed. A. F. C. Bourdillon, p. 91 (reprinted separately by the Family Welfare Association).

sellers', rhubarb and spice sellers, exhibitors of performing animals, organ-grinders, Punch and Judy shows, conjurers, street photographers, scavengers, mudlarks, sewer hunters, rat-catchers, chimney sweeps, coal heavers, lumpers and cabmen. Here was one of those 'two nations' into which, as Disraeli's *Sybil* had pointed out so dramatically, the English people was divided. Change was at work, but its task was far from finished: as G. M. Young has written, the 'conversion of the vast and shapeless city which Dickens knew – fog-bound and fever-haunted, brooding over its dark, mysterious river – into the imperial capital, of Whitehall, the Thames Embankment, and South Kensington, is the still visible symbol of the mid-Victorian transition'.[1]

A large part of the working people at this time – the vast, anonymous mass of 'the poor' – lived from week to week on the verge of poverty. Between them and starvation lay their weekly earnings. If these were cut off – whether through illness or old age or through 'slack trade' which caused many men to be laid off – the sources of help were few: begging, charity, the Poor Law. The state recognised to the poor one obligation only: to relieve the *destitute*, either in the work-house or by 'outdoor relief'. Of any other organisation for the relief of distress there was nothing: there were charities, but no organisation of charity.

The 1860's were a time of difficulty rather than depression: the cotton famine in Lancashire during the American Civil War, the failure of the Gurney and Overend Bank in 1866 when new railway construction was coming to an end as a stimulant of economic activity. Paupers (the number of persons receiving relief from the Poor Law authorities)

[1] G. M. Young, *Victorian England* (1936; second edition, 1953), p. 82. Cf. his 'The Happy Family' in *Last Essays* (1950). I have given a brief sketch of London in 'Charity and Casework in Late Victorian London: the work of the Charity Organisation Society', *Social Service Review*, 31: 258-9 (1957), reprinted in *Social Work* (1958).

numbered just over one million in England and Wales in 1863 and 1864, and again, after a slight fall, in 1869, 1870, 1871. The figure for 1871, 1,037,360 paupers, represented a ratio of 4·6 paupers per 100 of population, the total population being 22¾ millions. This figure was quite typical: in 1863 the ratio had been 5·3; in 1866, at its lowest, it was 4·3.

In London, the rate of pauperism was actually declining, but with the growth of the population the absolute number of paupers was increasing. In 1861, out of 2·8 million Londoners, 93,495 were in receipt of relief in a one-day count (March 25): in 1871, out of a population of 3·8 millions, the corresponding number of paupers was 142,371. At the same time the cost of relief in the country as a whole was increasing. In 1861 it was £5,778,943, or 5s. 9d. per head of population; in 1871 it was £7,886,724, or 6s. 11¼d. per head.[1]

These and other circumstances led to new thought about the Poor Law. Though many people (and they were to include many of the stalwarts of the C.O.S. in later times) were bitterly opposed to any liberalisation of the Poor Law or any compromise with the principle of 'less eligibility' which might encourage idleness and a recourse to the relieving officer, others were coming to see that destitution produced a variety of needs in relation to causes which made any single, rigorous kind of treatment quite unjustifiable. This was particularly true of medical relief; and it was largely as a result of inquiries into the workhouse infirmaries – wretchedly inadequate rooms, in which paupers and fellow-patients acted as nurses – that an important measure of reform was passed.

The Metropolitan Poor Act (1867) created a common poor fund for the Metropolis to which all unions contributed and from which a separate common service of hospitals and

[1] Local Government Board, 1st *Annual Report*, 1871-72, pp. ix, xxii, xiii.

asylums was provided by the Metropolitan Asylums Board; district Poor Law schools were also constructed under the Act. The maintenance of patients in the hospitals and asylums, of children in the district schools, and of vagrants, became a charge on the common poor fund, relieving the poorer unions of much of their responsibilities (and hence of an incentive to strict administration), and increasing the attractiveness of indoor relief. The report of the Poor Law Board for 1869-70 even raised the question 'how far it may be advisable, in a sanitary or social point of view, to extend gratuitous Medical Relief beyond the actual pauper class. . .'.[1] The threat to strict Poor Law principles which this implied was one stimulus to charity organisation, which, as we shall see, aimed at producing co-operation between charity and Poor Law in a joint campaign against poverty and dependence.

Another motive for the organisation of charity was the long-standing concern with the evils of street begging and of mendicity in general. In the 'sixties the plague of street beggars was still a grim reality. There were the crossing sweepers – generally harmless and tolerated. There were the tramps and cadgers, men and women who might intimidate a lady if she found herself confronted by one of them when walking alone in a quiet street. There were the children exhibited by their parents to excite pity by their rags and by sores deliberately produced. Begging had become a trade, and in the importunities of the writers of begging letters it was growing into a profession.

Out of this had sprung the anti-mendicity societies, whose objects were to prod the police into action against beggars and tramps, to investigate begging letters, and to relieve deserving cases by encouraging people to give, not money,

[1] Sidney and Beatrice Webb, *English Poor Law History*, Part II, vol. i (1929), p. 323.

but tickets entitling the recipient to a food order or a meal. One of the earliest of these was the Society for the Suppression of Public Begging, founded in Edinburgh in 1812. The principal one was the Society for the Suppression of Mendicity, founded in London in 1818. In a few counties (Ayr, Clackmannan, Dorset, Hereford) there were mendicity societies conducted under the auspices of the Chief Constable; in Gloucestershire, Wiltshire and Worcestershire these societies bore other titles, indicative of their main object, the suppression of vagrancy.

The Lancashire cotton famine reinforced the need for the organisation of charity by the new experience of relief schemes which it produced. To relieve the victims of the famine several relief funds were formed, totalling over £1 million in money collected in Great Britain, apart from generous contributions from Australia, the Northern states of America, and elsewhere. Manchester and Liverpool raised funds of their own; an appeal of the Lord Mayor of London produced the Mansion House Fund, a meeting at Bridgewater House (Lord Ellesmere's house in London) under the leadership of Lord Derby raised £52,000. Relief was distributed by local committees in each town, and with the co-operation of the Poor Law Guardians; but in spite of every care there were many cases of fraud and imposture.

We must, however, look elsewhere for the sort of concern with the problem of poverty, and the desire for a systematic means of relieving poverty, which inspired the organisation of charity.[1] Charity presupposed a class system, but one in which the fortunate accepted certain duties towards the

[1] Suggestive analyses of the social thought underlying the movement will be found in Karl de Schweinitz, *England's Road to Social Security* (Philadelphia, 1943), esp. ch. 14; A. F. Young and E. T. Ashton, *British Social Work in the Nineteenth Century* (1956); chapters by Una Cormack (already cited) and G. D. H. Cole in A. F. C. Bourdillon, *Voluntary Social Services*.

poorer classes: the sort of *noblesse oblige* which inspired
'Young England' and Disraeli's Egremont. The sense of
duty was strengthened in the middle classes by the evangelical
Christianity of the age. Even as late as 1897 a journalist
could entitle one chapter of his survey of the changes of the
Victorian Age 'Social Citizenship as a Moral Growth of
Victorian England'.[1] Christian Socialism as preached in the
1850's by J. M. Ludlow, F. D. Maurice and Charles Kingsley
stressed the importance of personal service to the poor as a
Christian duty, and the value of co-operative work.

Nor must we forget the feelings of uncertainty which
beset the educated classes in the 1860's. Darwin's *Origin of
Species* (1859) was perhaps less immediately disturbing to
old ideas about the order of nature and of society than
Essays and Reviews (1860) with its modernist, critical
approach to the Church and the scriptures. Mill's *Principles
of Political Economy* had argued that the country was
approaching a stationary state in which improvements in
the art of living and in distribution were more important
than progress on the side of production; in the third edition
of 1852 Mill had seemed to give a qualified approval to
socialism. His essay *On Liberty* (1859) had criticised *laissez-
faire* as the liberty of the privileged few; for the rest the only
liberty was the liberty to sell their labour or starve. Ruskin,
in *Unto this Last* (1862) was saying much the same thing:
'the "let alone" principle is in all things which man has to do
with the principle of death'. Work is the nation's wealth; 'it is
our inactivity . . . that ruins us'. Political economy based on
avarice and the desire for progress, rather than on justice
and affection, is false. 'The consummation of all wealth is in
the producing as many as possible full-breathed, bright-
eyed, and happy-hearted human creatures.'

[1] T. H. S. Escott, *Social Transformations of the Victorian Age*
(1897).

Background of Ideas and Founding of the C.O.S.

The decade of the 'sixties was also a period of rapid political change. The Reform Act of 1867 enfranchised most of the urban working men – one man in three had the vote after its passage; and it had been preceded by the great meetings, demonstrations and processions of the National Reform League and the alarming scenes outside Hyde Park in July 1866. At the same time the respectable working men were adding to their strength in the trade unions and trades councils. The first Trades Union Congress met in Manchester in 1868; and the agitation to improve the law relating to trade unions was to achieve success in the first Parliament elected on the new franchise. Two books published after the Reform Act expressed the doubts with which many people faced the new age. Matthew Arnold foresaw a new age of anarchy; the new sprawling democracy lacked any sense of direction beyond the worship of mammon and the complacent belief in material progress; only culture, the study of perfection, might redeem it (*Culture and Anarchy*, 1869). Similarly the second edition (1872) of Bagehot's *English Constitution* showed the greatest distrust of the new voters: they were unable to judge of intellectual matters; would they defer to wealth and rank as the old electors had done, or try instead to create a 'poor man's paradise'?

It was in this setting that people turned to consider anew the condition of their less fortunate neighbours. One form of personal service which they could give, and which had grown sporadically in the towns, was friendly visiting, house-to-house visits to the homes of the poor. This had been organised as early as 1788 in Hamburg into a means of relieving poverty throughout the city. A common fund was raised by weekly collections and taxation; the town was divided into districts, in which citizens visited persons in need and investigated their cases; relief was given when the need was proved, but work was exacted in return; a hospital and a day nursery

The Charity Organisation Society

were provided. A pamphlet by one of the leaders, Baron Kaspar van Voght, *Letter to Some Friends of the Poor in Great Britain*, published in 1796 and republished in 1817, made the experiment known to British reformers.[1]

It was a system of this sort that was put into effect in Glasgow in 1819 by Dr Thomas Chalmers (later the leader of the Free Church secession from the Church of Scotland) in his parish of St John's. Elders and deacons of the church were the visitors and investigators, carrying out the ideal of neighbourliness and aiding those in need with funds raised in church. The scheme had lapsed by 1837, but it was well known through Chalmers' writings, and he became almost the patron saint of the C.O.S.[2] The 'Elberfeld system' was another German experiment which became known in England. Elberfeld, a town of 100,000 in the Rhine Province of Prussia, had instituted a system of relief in 1852, using almoners in 26 districts of the town to visit applicants for help and report their cases to a fortnightly meeting of the district almoners for decision. Relief, when given, came partly from public funds and partly from charitable endowments. The almoners were unpaid, but their service was compulsory for a three-year term.

In London the idea of friendly visiting attracted several persons who were prominent in the later history of the C.O.S. In 1843 Charles Blomfield, the Bishop of London, and others founded the Metropolitan Visiting and Relief Association or, to give it its full title, the Association for Promoting the Relief of Destitution, and for Improving the Condition of the Poor, by means of Parochial and District Visiting, under the superintendence and direction of the Bishops and Clergy, through the Agency of Unpaid Visitors, and without reference to religious persuasion. The M.V.R.A. made use of case

[1] K. de Schweinitz, *op. cit.*, pp. 91-4.
[2] *Ibid.*, ch. 11.

· 10 ·

papers of a sort from the first. Each visitor had two forms, 'V', the District Visitor's Report to the local committee on families helped, and 'V1', 'Page of District Visitor's Journal'.[1] In 1860 the Society for the Relief of Distress was founded to help the poor of the London parishes; its members were voluntary almoners who visited those in need before help was given.

One of the almoners of the S.R.D. was Edward Denison. In 1867, not satisfied with mere visiting, he went to live for eight months in a poor district in Philpot Street, Mile End Road. Well connected (the son of a bishop) and well endowed with friends, he poured out his ideas in private letters and served briefly as a Member of Parliament before his early death, in his thirtieth year, in 1870. He deplored the absence in the East End of any class of well-to-do and leisured people who could give help to the less fortunate; he deplored 'subscription charity' and the effects of indiscriminate giving and of lax Poor Law administration, particularly in outdoor relief. He advocated the organisation of charity, and joined in a plan for co-operation between the Guardians and private charity in Mile End. He believed that most of the poor would be able to 'tide over the occasional months of want of work or of sickness' if they were frugal and thrifty. His ideas foreshadow, in fact, almost the whole of the philosophy and practice of the C.O.S.[2]

Another man who combined a spirit of compassion with a belief that the efficiency of charity could be improved by

[1] J. C. Pringle, *Social work of the London Churches: Being some account of the Metropolitan Visiting and Relief Association, 1843-1937* (1937), p. 184. This lively book tells more of its author (for many years Secretary of the C.O.S.) than of its subject, and is not always entirely accurate.

[2] *Work among the London Poor: Letters and Other Writings of the late Edward Denison*, ed. Sir Baldwyn Leighton, Bart. (cheap edition, 1884), esp. pp. 42, 61-3, 79, 84, 134, 163, 245. This tribute to Denison's memory was first published in 1872.

better organisation was William Rathbone of Liverpool, remarkable member of a remarkable family. He founded in Liverpool the District Nursing Society in 1859; this in turn led to the Liverpool Training School and Home for Nurses, begun in 1862. Even more important was his campaign against indiscriminate charity as encouraging pauperisation and fraud, and his work for charity organisation. He persuaded the three chief charitable societies in Liverpool to amalgamate in 1863 as the Central Relief Society. In 1867 he published his *Social Duties, considered in Reference to the Organisation of Effort in Works of Benevolence and Public Utility*.[1]

Similar ideas were nurtured by Charles B. P. Bosanquet, who was to give yeoman service to the C.O.S. as its first secretary. He was by profession a barrister, a member of a landed family of Huguenot descent whose seat was at Rock, near Alnwick, Northumberland. He had given much of his time to friendly visiting, and in 1868 published *London: some account of its Growth, Charitable Agencies, and Wants*. It contained chapters dealing with modern London and its 'Sunken Sixth', religious agencies and charitable societies, the working classes, sanitary legislation, the dwellings of the poor, overcrowding, model housing, the Poor Law, the parochial system; it described Dr Chalmers' work in Glasgow, the Elberfeld system, and poor relief in Paris and New York – examples frequently cited by the C.O.S. subsequently; and it recounted some of the author's personal experiences in district visiting in the chapter of 'Suggestions to Laymen'.

In these years another pioneer of social work, one of the most remarkable women of Victorian England, was gaining experience by her own extraordinary 'inner-directed' work.

---

[1] See Margaret B. Simey, *Charitable Effort in Liverpool in the Nineteenth Century* (Liverpool, 1951), and Eleanor Rathbone, *William Rathbone: a memoir* (1905).

Background of Ideas and Founding of the C.O.S.

Octavia Hill, granddaughter of the great public health worker, Dr Southwood Smith, had stumbled against the facts of poverty while in her teens, when directing the work of poor children in a short-lived Co-operative Guild. She and her mother and sisters began inviting in the neighbouring women of poor families to their house one evening a week, for sewing and sociability. Her friendship with F. D. Maurice encouraged her inclination toward social work, but it was Ruskin, to whom she went for painting lessons, who gave it a practical direction by buying three working-class houses in Paradise Place, Marylebone, for her to manage. This was in 1865, when she was 27. She has been well called 'the first professional case-worker',[1] for in these houses and the many others which she came to manage she worked out and applied the principles of housing management as a part of social work. She and her 'fellow-workers' – women whom she trained in voluntary service on her principles – were rent-collectors who were also friendly visitors, whose care it was to get to know 'their' families and to help them not only by providing decent housing but by advice in their personal problems and by the encouragement of thrift (they collected their tenants' savings and managed a savings fund). As early as November 1866 she explained her work in the *Fortnightly Review*: it combined a good landlady's duties towards her tenants and the friendship 'which grows up from intimate knowledge'. Her ideas anticipated those of the C.O.S., of which she became one of the first members and in later days a staunch defender.[2]

Octavia Hill's work touched another of the springs of

[1] Una Cormack, *loc. cit.*, p. 97.

[2] The best life of Octavia Hill is by E. Moberley Bell (1942); see also the work of her sister's husband, C. E. Maurice, *The Life of Octavia Hill as told in her Letters* (1913), and her essays in *Homes of the London Poor* (New York, 1875) and *Our Common Land* (1877). W. T. Hill, *Octavia Hill* (1956), is unsatisfactory.

charity and charity organisation. Thrift was part of the great network of self-help by which the respectable Victorian working men bettered their position: savings banks, friendly societies, trade unions, mechanics' institutes, co-operative societies. Samuel Smiles published *Self-Help* in 1859. Ultimately self-help and charity might be in conflict; in the 1860's the one inspired the other with the belief that the poor could be helped, by intelligent charity, to help themselves.

Last but by no means least in the background of ideas was the conviction, reinforced by every new invention and scientific discovery, that any problem, such as the problem of poverty, could be solved by study, thought, the ascertaining of the facts, the application of scientific method. The work of the statistical societies, first founded in London, Manchester and Bristol in the 1830's, pointed in this direction. Equally influential for a time was the National Association for the Promotion of Social Science (often known as the Social Science Association), founded in 1857 under the patronage of Lord Brougham, in imitation of the British Association for the Advancement of Science. Until its demise in 1886 its annual meetings were great occasions for the discussion of social questions, and its published Transactions a repository of facts, experience, theory. It was organised in five departments: law amendment, education, prevention and repression of crime, public health, and social economy – the last comprising questions of capital, labour and production.[1]

In this setting the C.O.S. was born, not without some difficulty, in 1869. Its origins are hard to discover: for a pamphlet on its history, written as early as 1874, provoked four rejoinders and an unsuccessful appeal to the Council of

[1] Brian Rodgers, 'The Social Science Association, 1857-1886' *Manchester School of Economics and Social Studies*, XX (1952), 283-310.

the Society for a decision on the question of origins. It is clear that the ideas behind it had long been in the air, and trace back at least to the founding of the Society for the Relief of Distress in 1860. An early member of this society, G. M. Hicks, read a paper to it in February 1861 in which he advocated the establishment of district offices staffed by almoners who would investigate applications for help and would co-operate with the Poor Law authorities. Nothing came of this except a sub-committee's endorsement, but Hicks returned to the subject in March 1868 in a letter to the *Pall Mall Gazette* outlining a plan for a central board of charities to make an annual report on all charities and to audit their accounts. An article by J. R. Green on poverty in the East End, in the *Saturday Review* for December 28, 1867, had emphasised the chaos of numerous competing charities whose unco-ordinated efforts often served to increase mendicancy and pauperism.[1]

Matters moved forward in June 1868, when a paper was read at a meeting of the Society of Arts, under the chairmanship of A. C. Tait, the Bishop of London, with the title 'How to deal with the Unemployed Poor of London and with its "Roughs" and Criminal Classes'. Its author was Henry Solly (1813-1903), son of a Baltic timber merchant of London, a Congregational minister who was for a few years the secretary of the Working Men's Club and Institute Union after its founding in 1862, and was later interested in the subject of industrial villages.[2] The paper contained little or nothing about charity organisation, and would be of no importance to us except that it led to plans for starting a society.

[1] Cited in Karl de Schweinitz, *England's Road to Social Security*, p. 145.
[2] See the sketch of him in Lord Beveridge, *Voluntary Action* (1948), pp. 168-70, citing Solly's *These Eighty Years* (2 vols., 1893) and his *Working Men's Clubs* (2nd ed., 1904).

On October 31 a prospectus – one among several rivals – was framed for an Association for the Prevention of Pauperism and Crime; among other proposals it recommended co-operation between the Poor Law and private charity for the purpose of helping those in distress to help themselves. Solly's efforts to enlist support for this society were unavailing, though several meetings of an executive committee were held.

On December 17, 1868, another meeting was held at the Society of Arts under these auspices, with Lord Shaftesbury in the chair. At this a paper was read by Thomas Hawksley, M.D.[1] on 'The Charities of London and Some Errors in their Administration: with Suggestions for an Improved System of Private and Official Charitable Relief'. Hawksley touched upon the increase of pauperism, the failure of the Poor Law to investigate cases, the lack of system in the administration of charities and the opportunities for fraud which this entailed. He wanted all charities to agree to receive applications for help only through a single office of registration or inquiry in each parish or district, under the supervision of a central office and with powers of audit. The scheme was to be financed by a tax of 1 per cent. on the income of the London charities. Following this meeting a new prospectus was issued on December 29 and further meetings were held in the new year, attended by Solly, Hawksley, Captain (later Admiral) F. A. Maxse, Lord Lichfield, General Sir Orfeur Cavenagh, W. M. Wilkinson and others.

The next step was the holding of a conference of representatives of Metropolitan charities on February 11, 1869.

---

[1] Hawksley, who died in 1892 at the age of 71, founded in 1885 the Destitute Boys National School of Handicrafts at Chertsey. He had a large practice in London and Brighton and was physician at Margaret Street Consumption and Chest Diseases Hospital.

Background of Ideas and Founding of the C.O.S.

Hawksley read his paper, which provoked, not unnaturally, a vigorous debate and no agreement. Following this W. M. Wilkinson drew up a paper with the object of drawing different ideas together: Hicks later claimed that its proposals were his, and that he had read a similar paper at a meeting at Lord Lichfield's house; it is clear that he, Solly, Hawksley and no doubt several others contributed the ideas on which the C.O.S. was eventually founded. One contributor was the Rev. Martyn Hart, later Dean of Denver, Colorado, who had devised a system of mendicity tickets in his parish of Blackheath. Wilkinson's plan, if his it was, contained the basis of the subsequent work of the C.O.S.: inquiry into all applications for help, district offices, co-operation with the Poor Law.

Other meetings of a small committee followed, with Lord Lichfield taking a prominent part in them. It was he who took steps to find a home for the society, asking his private secretary, C. J. Ribton-Turner, to hire an office and furnish it at his expense. Ribton-Turner obtained rooms on the first floor of 15 Buckingham Street, Adelphi, on March 22, and there for many years the C.O.S. had its headquarters.[1]

The final step was taken at a meeting on April 29, 1869. On Wilkinson's motion the society took the name of the Society for Organising Charitable Relief and Repressing Mendicity: the shorter and familiar name, the Charity Organisation Society was, however, used almost from the first. The C.O.S. was thus an outgrowth of the abortive Society for the Prevention of Pauperism and Crime, and the new name and to some extent the new character which it took was largely due to Lord Lichfield's intervention. Lord

[1] Buckingham Street was (and is) a quiet street running down to the old Water Gate of York House (now in the Victoria Embankment Gardens). A slight etching of the Water Gate graced the title page of C.O.S. publications. No. 15 no longer stands: a new building was erected on its site in 1908.

The Charity Organisation Society

Lichfield was the first chairman; G. M. Hicks, Alsager Hay Hill, C. J. Ribton-Turner and Charles B. P. Bosanquet shared the duties of honorary secretary. After July 1870, Bosanquet was secretary; Ribton-Turner continued as organising secretary. The C.O.S. had been established, and within a year had grown into a large, vigorous and impressive body.[1]

[1] This account rests on that written by E. C. Price, assistant secretary of the C.O.S., in the *Charity Organisation Review*, VIII, 355-72 (October-November 1892); see also *C. O. Review*, February 1892 (letter of C. B. P. Bosanquet), February 1896 (12: 57-58) and March 1896 p. 112. There are good brief accounts of the C.O.S. by W. A. Bailward in the *Quarterly Review*, January 1907 (206: 55-76), and by Karl de Schweinitz, *England's Road to Social Security*, ch. 14. The standard work, not entirely satisfactory, is Helen Bosanquet, *Social Work in London, 1869 to 1912: A History of the Charity Organisation Society* (1914).

CHAPTER II

The District Committees and the Practice of Casework

The scale on which the new society was projected, and something of the future character of its work, can be seen in the first annual report of the Council of the C.O.S. The report was presented at the first annual meeting, held, as often in later years, at Willis's Rooms, on March 30, 1870. The Earl of Derby was in the chair. The report lists a most imposing array of names. The President is the Bishop of London, the Chairman, Lord Lichfield, and the Council includes the Marquess of Westminster, Lord Vernon, Lord George Hamilton, M.P., Major-General Cavenagh, Archbishop Manning, G. P. Bidder, Q.C.,[1] F. J. S. Edgcombe, W. E. Gladstone, M.P., Sir John Gorst, Dr Hawksley, Octavia Hill, Sir Baldwyn Leighton, Captain Maxse, F. D. Mocatta, John Ruskin, W. H. Smith, M.P., the Right Honourable W. Cowper-Temple, M.P., Sir Charles Trevelyan, the Rev. M. S. A. Walrond (for many years hon. secretary of the Metropolitan Relief and Visiting Association), W. M. Wilkinson and J. Hornsby Wright. The total membership of the Council was 54.

To some extent the C.O.S. always went in for skilful window-dressing. In the second annual report the category or vice-president appears, and includes twenty-four men: the Dukes of Norfolk and Northumberland, the Marquesses

---

[1] Son of G. P. Bidder, the famous 'calculating boy' and engineer.

of Camden, Lansdowne, Salisbury and Westminster, the Earl of Derby, two lesser peers, Manning, Lord George Hamilton, Goschen, Ruskin, W. H. Smith and Cowper-Temple. This list changed only with additions for several years (Lord Shaftesbury, for example); in 1880 it included 17 peers. Most of the vice-presidents took little active part in the work of the Society beyond lending it the support of their names and purses. It was the Council, a larger if less distinguished body, which contained the real leaders of the C.O.S. (after the first year most of the great names were transferred from the Council to the list of vice-presidents). Yet the enlisting of great names which appeared in all the Society's publications was part of the Society's method and its strength. It was a propagandist body, and must give all the weight it could to its utterances and its work. Names helped in this, the more influential the better. In the fourth report the Queen appears as the Society's Patron.

Apart from members of the Council, whom we shall notice later, the two men who contributed most to the early growth of the C.O.S. and to its permanent character were the two secretaries, C. B. P. Bosanquet and C. J. Ribton-Turner. Bosanquet's impress is clear, both in the organisation of the Central Office and the Council, and in the theory and practice of casework which, through the District Committees, immediately became the Society's main work. He resigned in 1875 to assume the management of his family estate. To no one did the C.O.S. owe more in its formative years. Ribton-Turner was organising secretary until 1877. Thereafter he devoted himself to a large historical work, *Vagrants and Vagrancy: and Beggars and Begging*, which traced the history of vagrancy and mendicancy in Great Britain and in continental Europe from the earliest times. It was published in 1887, and dedicated to Lord Lichfield. It was due to him that the work of establishing the District Committees of the C.O.S. was accomplished as expeditiously and completely as it was, in less than two years' time.

The plan of the C.O.S., as presented in its first report, was to establish in each Poor Law division a Charity Office under the management of a local Committee. The office was to be staffed by a Charity Agent, who was to be in direct communication with the Poor Law Relieving Officer and with the clergy and all the charities and charity societies within the district. The Agent was to keep a register of 'all cases relieved by the several charitable agencies in the district'. He was to 'inquire into and investigate, and, if necessary, in the last resort, assist, under the instructions of the Committee, such special cases as cannot be met by existing agencies, referring, however, all cases which may be met by such agencies to their appropriate channels of relief'. The office was thus intended to be the 'recognised centre of charitable organisation' in the district. Printed tickets were issued, and persons were urged to give these, rather than money, to beggars and other needy persons; these tickets to be presented by the recipients at the local office.[1]

District Offices of this sort received an early blessing from the government and might well have developed into semi-official agencies. On November 20, 1869, the Poor Law Board under the presidency of G. J. Goschen issued the 'Goschen Minute' on 'The Relief of the Poor in the Metropolis'. It discussed the question 'how far it is possible to mark out the separate limits of the Poor Law and of charity respectively, and how it is possible to secure joint action between the two'. The Poor Law should, it argued, confine itself to the destitute, leaving to charity the task of helping the poor, for example by supplementing a widow's small earnings, for helping a man

---

[1] C.O.S. 1st *Report of the Council*, 1870, and 'Rough Sketch of Proposed Plan' included with it.

in distress by redeeming his goods from pawn, or providing
him with tools or clothes or the means of travel to a new
job – all things the Poor Law was debarred from doing. It
recommended that there should be a 'public registering
office' in every district, in order that every agency, charitable
or public, should know what the others were doing, and it
urged the charitable bodies not to help persons relieved by
the Poor Law, and to report those whom they assisted to the
relieving officer. The Guardians, on their side, would be
permitted to furnish to the office a weekly list of persons
receiving relief from them.[1]

With this encouragement, the C.O.S. opened District
Offices with remarkable speed. Offices were open in twelve
Poor Law divisions by the time the first annual report was
issued in March 1870; in the third annual report, for 1871, it
was stated that there were thirty District Committees,
embracing every division except that of the City of London.
The total number of District Offices in 1872 was 36, some
divisions having more than one, while in other cases
one office served more than one division. In the East
End there was one office, that of the East End Inquiry
Committee, opened in February 1871, and serving five
divisions; it was not until 1875 that each of these had its own
committee.

From the very start, however, the District Offices failed
of their first purpose, that of co-ordinating the work of all
the local charities and the Poor Law and of registering and
directing all applicants for aid. Such a large scheme, overrid-
ing the charitable work of the clergy, ministers and societies,
often strong rivals of each other, could hardly succeed, and
the second annual report of the C.O.S. was constrained to

[1] Text in *22nd Annual Report of the Poor Law Board*, 1869-70,
pp. 9-12; Thomas Mackay, *History of the English Poor Law* (vol. III
of Sir George Nicholls' *History*; 1899), pp. 501-4.

admit that 'an ideal of this sort was not to be realised at once'. In fact it never was. The District Committees were purely C.O.S. Committees, though they often included persons who were also members of other societies, and they often referred applicants to other agencies for help. The registers of the District Offices were of their own cases only, nor, except briefly in one instance, was any official co-operation with the Poor Law achieved.

The one brief exception was in Marylebone, where the first District Committee was started in May 1869 by the vicar of St Mary's, the Hon. and Rev. W. Fremantle, later Dean of Ripon. This was Octavia Hill's home ground, and here she put her ideas of charity into practice. Another influential and devoted supporter was Colonel (later General) Sir Lynedoch Gardiner, honorary secretary of the District Committee and a Poor Law Guardian. He had seen service at Court, and was active in the work of the Moore Street Home for Crippled Boys.[1] In the division of St Mary's, Bryanston Square, Octavia Hill organised a body of district visitors, ultimately 35 in number, working on C.O.S. principles under the District Committee. Alongside was another committee, the St Mary's Relief Committee, using the charitable funds in the control of Fremantle, the vicar. All applications for help from the Relief Committee were referred to the district visitors for inquiry, and help was given only in accordance with their findings; Octavia Hill was a member of both bodies, and served as referee and 'personal link' between both. In the winter of 1872-73 the Poor Law Guardians agreed to give Miss Hill a daily list of applicants for relief from her district. The appropriate district visitor made a report on each applicant, which was returned to the relieving officer 'who uses it as he may see fit'. The Guardians' decisions in these cases were

[1] See the obituary notice in *Charity Organisation Review*, February 1898.

subsequently transmitted to her in a weekly report.[1] In 1875 the system was extended into a second district.[2] Thereafter, the plan seems to have lapsed, judging from the silence of the Marylebone committee's reports, though there continued to be good relations between the Guardians and the District Committee, and the relieving officer often referred cases to the Committee and vice versa.[3]

Out of this failure of its original purpose the C.O.S. plucked success in another direction. It had in its original plan instructed the Agent of the District Office to 'investigate, and, if necessary, in the last resort, assist . . . such special cases as cannot be met by existing agencies' (p. 21, *sup.*). With the failure of charity organisation, the assistance of special cases, and not merely in the last resort, became the main business of the District Offices. This, coupled as it was with the careful investigation of each application before help was given, put the C.O.S. fairly and squarely into social and family casework. In its second report in 1871 the Council of the C.O.S. admitted that they had 'felt themselves obliged, by the nature of the case, to advise the committees to give relief themselves in the last resort'.

What was the 'nature of the case' which took the C.O.S. into casework? It was partly that in the poorer districts,

[1] The reports of Octavia Hill and Colonel Lynedoch Gardiner on this scheme of co-operation between Guardians and voluntary agencies are in the 3rd *Annual Report of the Local Government Board*, 1873-74, pp. 126-35. See also the annual reports of the Marylebone Committee of the C.O.S. for 1873 and 1874. Octavia Hill gave a briefer account in her paper on 'The work of volunteers in the organisation of charity', printed in her *Homes of the London Poor* (New York, 1875), pp. 53-8. See also E.M. Bell, *Octavia Hill*, pp. 109-11.

[2] Marylebone Committee, C.O.S., *Annual Report* for 1875.

[3] See, especially, Marylebone Committee *Report* for 1881. Other annual reports of the time, e.g., for 1876, 1878, 1885, 1886, merely refer to co-operation between the Committee and the Guardians in general terms. For other examples of co-operation between the C.O.S. and the Poor Law see Chapter VI.

where the need was greatest, there were few charitable societies at work. But much more it was the principles of charity to which the C.O.S. was committing itself, and which it could realise only by practising them in actual cases.

Perhaps the earliest statement of the C.O.S. idea of charity – that it must help, not harm, and be a work of friendly neighbourliness – is a private one. In 1869 Octavia Hill read a paper to the Social Science Association with the significant title 'The Importance of aiding the poor without almsgiving'. She argued that man's spirit was more important than his material prosperity; any gift which did not make a man better, stronger, more independent, damaged rather than helped him.[1] The C.O.S.'s own statement, in its second report, ran:

> To give material relief, food or money, to everyone who asked for it on the sole conditions of their being what is commonly called deserving and in want, even after the most careful verification of those conditions, would inevitably do more harm than good, though this might not be seen during the first year or two.[2]

The plainest statement of C.O.S. principles appeared in the annual report for 1875.

The aim of the Society is to improve the condition of the poor, upon the following definite principles:

1. Systematic co-operation with Poor Law authorities, charitable agencies, and individuals.

2. Careful investigation of applications for charitable aid, by competent officers, each case being duly considered, after inquiry, by a Committee of experienced

[1] E. Moberly Bell, *Octavia Hill*, p. 108; C. E. Maurice, *Life of Octavia Hill*, p. 258.

[2] C.O.S., 2nd *Annual Report*, 1870 (presented March 22, 1871), p. 5.

volunteers, including representatives of the principal local charities and religious denominations.

3. Judicious and effectual assistance in all deserving cases, either through the aid of existing agencies, or, failing these, from the funds of the Society; those cases that cannot be properly dealt with by charity being left to the Guardians.

4. The promotion of habits of providence and self-reliance, and of those social and sanitary principles, the observance of which is essential to the well-being of the poor and of the community at large.

5. The repression of mendicity and imposture, and the correction of the maladministration of charity.

It is desirable that it should be distinctly understood that it is the chief aim of the Society to deal with the causes of pauperism rather than with its effects, and permanently to elevate the condition of the poor by the application of the above principles, combined with pecuniary or other material assistance.[1]

Another exposition is to be found in the report of a District Committee in 1876:

The principle is, that it is good for the poor that they should meet all the *ordinary* contingencies of life, relying not upon public or private charity, but upon their own industry and thrift, and upon the powers of self-help that are to be developed by individual and collective effort. Ample room will still be left for the exercise of an abundant charity in dealing with exceptional misfortune, and also in connection with large schemes for the benefit of the working classes which may require, in the first instance at all events, the fostering of wealth and leisure. But it is a hurtful misuse of money to spend it in assisting the

[1] 5th *Annual Report*, 1875, pp. 5-6.

District Committees and Practice of Casework

labouring classes to meet emergencies which they should themselves have anticipated and provided for.[1]

One more statement, dating from 1889, may be given:

That acts of charity may produce well-being, the utmost care must be taken to strengthen the moral nature of the individual who may be in distress, and to call out for his aid the sympathy and assistance of his family and those upon whom he is in any way dependent. Everything should be done to help distress in such a way that it does not become a matter rather of public than of private concern; that it is met, and, if possible, prevented, within the private circle of family and friends.[2]

The application of these principles through casework was the responsibility of the District Committees. Each committee consisted of a chairman, often a man of title, and a large number of members, including some of the local clergy and ministers. There was an honorary secretary (sometimes more than one) and an honorary treasurer. In some districts responsibility was delegated to smaller committees: a finance committee, an administrative committee, a decision committee; Paddington in 1873 had a finance committee, and three working committees meeting on Mondays, Wednesdays and Fridays respectively. An office was maintained: Paddington's was open daily from 10 to 12 and 3 to 5.

The daily work of a District Office was partly done by volunteers – mainly women; but it is important to notice as one of the distinctive features of the C.O.S. that a paid staff was employed in casework from the first: sometimes this consisted of an Agent, but the larger committees had one or two other employees, called Collectors, Enquirers, Inquiry

[1] Extract from the Annual Report of a District Committee, reprinted as Appendix IV of the 8th *Annual Report* of the C.O.S., 1876, p. 24. The entire passage is an extreme statement of the C.O.S. philosophy: see Appendix at end of this chapter.

[2] 21st *Annual Report*, 1889, p. 2.

Agents. We hear little of these officers: they were men of the working class, and in some committees' lists were distinguished from the members, who were designated Esquire, by appearing simply as Mr W. Harris or Mr Holligan or (appropriately enough) as Mr Welfare. One who subsequently became famous was Harry Snell, a village boy from Nottinghamshire who was paid Inquiry Agent for Woolwich in 1890. He was a Labour M.P. from 1922 to 1931, when he was made Lord Snell, Under-Secretary of State for India; from 1934 to 1938 he was chairman of the London County Council. His career with the C.O.S. lasted for some five years, but he found the Society's views of charity too narrow, though he praised its casework. He was fortunate in having a chief who by C.O.S. standards was unorthodox and overgenerous, C. H. Grinling.[1] The salaries paid such men in 1887 were usually about 30s. per week (£78 per year), though some were less, such as £1 a week or, evidently for part-time work, 5s. a week; on the other hand the Agent in St Georges-in-the-East received £138, 1s. 6d. In a few cases the Collector was paid poundage on subscriptions: the highest was £36, 13s. 2d., paid to the Paddington Committee's Collector.

In its work the District Committee was not left to its own unaided inspiration. The Council of the C.O.S. published both papers for its guidance and forms and registers for its use. 'Charity Organisation and Relief, A Paper of suggestions for Charity Organisation Societies', first published in 1880, laid down twelve principles of relief: each case must be treated separately; the welfare of the whole family must be considered; full inquiry must be made as to the causes of distress, needs, resources, character; temporary help should be given only if it will result in permanent benefit, not merely because the applicants are respectable and 'deserving'; thrift should be encouraged and repayment of help

[1] See Snell's autobiographical *Men, Movements and Myself* (1936).

required if possible; and the assistance of friends and relatives should be sought. 'Personal help should bear a large proportion to material aid.'[1] This was one of eleven papers in *Charity Organisation Papers*, which was first issued in 1881. Several were very old. No. 1, 'General Objects, Constitution, and Method of the C.O.S.', had appeared as 'District Committee Papers, No. 1' as early as October 1871. No. 2 in that same series was the paper on Loans, No. 4 was on Books and Forms, No. 5 was the paper on suggested by-laws, and an unnumbered paper in the same series was entitled 'Regulations for the Conduct of Inquiries at Offices of the Council'. The paper on 'The Necessity for repressing Vagrancy and Mendicity' then appeared as 'County Paper No. 9'.[2] 'Principles of Decision', No. 5 of the 1881 series, had first appeared as 'School Board Cases' in 1878.

'Books and Forms' is important for the development of C.O.S. methods in casework. It recommended that all applications should be taken down on a Visiting Form, and names and details entered, and a number assigned to each case, in the Record Book; after investigation, the case should be entered in the Decision Book. A Register and Index Book was also to be kept, as the register of relief given by all the local charities. Besides the Visiting Form there were forms for subscribers, for reports to subscribers, for inquiries to schoolmasters and to employers. The books and forms could be obtained at Messrs Johnson and Co., 121 Fleet Street, at the prices listed.[3]

[1] Charity Organisation Paper No. 2, in *Charity Organisation Papers*, first published in 1881; later revised editions in 1896 and 1907. The issuing of Paper No. 2 is mentioned in *Charity Organisation Reporter*, March 4, 1880.

[2] In bound volume lettered 'D.C. Papers &c' in C.O.S. library. All these date from 1870 to 1875.

[3] Slight changes in procedure will be found in the revised editions of 'Books and Forms' in 1872 and 1875. Loan forms, loan ledgers and receipt books, and collector's receipt books were added.

Besides these papers there were the lengthier manuals. *Suggestions for Systematic Inquiry into the Cases of Applicants for Relief*, by C. J. Ribton-Turner, published by Knight & Company, Fleet Street, at 2s. 6d., was in existence before May 1872. This was the forerunner of C. B. P. Bosanquet's *Visitors' Handy-book*, published by Longmans for the Council in 1874, and the several editions of *How to Help Cases of Distress*, taken from the introduction to the C.O.S. *Annual Charities Register and Digest*, and first published separately in 1883.

With the aid of these books and forms, and the innumerable case histories which the C.O.S. published to attract subscribers and illustrate its methods, we can reconstruct the casework of a District Office. The first step was the taking down of the case, in correct style, by someone, probably a voluntary worker, in the District Office to which the applicant had come. The Applicant and Decision Book had space for entering particulars of an applicant's employment, past addresses, relatives, membership of clubs, rent, articles in pawn, health; and the replies to inquiries of employers, the clergy, schoolmasters and others could be entered later in the appropriate places. Inquiries were then made, on the basis of the applicant's statements, by post or by interview; and the applicant's home was visited, either by the Committee's Agent or by a voluntary worker.

In due course the case would be written up and a decision made by the District Committee or a sub-committee: rejection, referred to some other charity or the Poor Law, or a plan of help. A loan or grant might be made, a mangle provided, a place in a convalescent home found, a pension arranged for. More visits to the family followed – once a week, if possible, by the worker whose case it had become – until it was clear that the family had been restored to independence and self-support (or that it was beyond help). The time and trouble which such a method entailed is hard for us of the present age to imagine: the number of calls to be made, on foot, the repeated visits at awkward hours if it was necessary to track down some elusive person, the letters to be written, often fruitlessly if false or incomplete addresses were given. Yet without this, investigation and verification were impossible; more important, the personal interest, the getting to know the distressed family so that it could be helped to help itself – all that true charity involved – would have been unattainable.

The kind of help given varied with each case. Would-be emigrants were assisted by grants, sometimes to purchase outfits. Small traders and artisans were helped by loans: a gardener to buy seeds, a shopkeeper to paint his tobacco shop, another man to purchase a scythe. Widows were often provided with mangles or sewing machines so that they might take in work and become self-supporting. A young woman was given money to buy clothes 'in order to take up a permanent situation'. A waterman was helped to get his son apprenticed, a carpenter with his fare to go to employment offered him in Yorkshire. A sick mother or child might be sent to a convalescent home, a crippled boy be given a surgical boot from a surgical aid society. If fatherless children needed care, relatives might be asked to take them in. Since the main concern was to preserve the family, strengthen character and encourage thrift and self-support, help was often given by loan (the necessity of regular repayments, probably to a weekly visitor, was itself an encouragement to thrift). If money was given, for example to old people, the attempt would be made to raise the needed sum from grown-up children, other relatives, or former employers; individual donors might also be sought out.

The types of cases helped by the District Committees in the early days can be seen from the annual report of the

Fulham and Hammersmith Committee for 1873.[1] A loan was given to a man of 29, a boot-closer, whose earnings were insufficient to support his wife and four children, to enable the family to purchase a sewing machine by which to supplement his earnings. An old couple who gained their living by a horse and cart were given a loan to buy a new horse, the old one having become lame and been shot: 'this deserving old couple [was given] a fresh start in life, and they were thus enabled to keep their own home over their heads instead of becoming recipients of parish relief'. A painter who had had to pawn clothes and bedding when out of work for eleven weeks was given a grant of £1 to support his wife and four children; and a labourer with an equally large family was given a small grant after he had pawned his clothes for food. Two other families were helped to emigrate.

In appealing for support, the C.O.S. relied heavily on the effect of case histories, given in full. Its annual reports are full of them, and many more appeared in the *Charity Organisation Review* in advertisements asking for a particular sum for each case. This technique had two advantages; it aroused sympathy, and, even more important, it was educational. One example, an Islington case of 1883, may be instructive:

> R. B., a widow with three children, also came before the Committee as a Poor Law case. She asked to have her children placed in a school, but as she was receiving out-relief, this could not be undertaken. It transpired during the consideration of the case that she had a pension of £10 per annum on account of her husband's good character – a sum of course inadequate to keep her, but yet sufficient

[1] The annual reports of the District Committees were published separately: the C.O.S. library bound together the reports of them all, annually. The reports were often cited in the annual reports of the Council; those for 1884 were included in the 16th *Annual Report* of the Council (1884).

to disqualify her from Poor Law aid. A Guardian being present, took note of this, and her relief was stopped. She then appeared to be worse off than when she applied to the Society. Being, however, no longer a pauper, and barred by her slender annuity from becoming so in future, there was no longer any objection to private aid being extended to her. Her character was excellent; the only difficulty was how to enable her to earn sufficient to support herself and children independently. One of the ladies of the Committee visited her and thought her so well calculated for a nurse, that training for this was suggested to her; she expressed her readiness to follow this advice if her children could be placed comfortably in schools or in a family. Various efforts were made in this direction without success. At last, a gentleman who had known her husband in the army and respected him, procured admission for the eldest to a Military School; a home in the country, near a good day school, was found for the two others, the mother giving her annuity as part payment, and the Committee promising to find the rest for the first year. Then the mother applied to St Thomas's Hospital to be trained as a nurse: but here alas, came a new difficulty! The time of hardship she had gone through while on out-relief, had so weakened her, that she could not satisfy the medical requirement of strength. So the lady already interested in her, found for her a situation in a family as a children's nurse, where it is hoped that good food and comparative freedom from toil and anxiety will restore her strength and enable her to undertake the more highly paid work, for which, in all other respects, she appeared so well fitted. This case is by no means an exceptional instance of the care bestowed by the Society on their work. It took nearly eight months before it was brought to a satisfactory conclusion; it involved interviews, considerable correspondence, the expenditure of about £20; yet is not this more truly to 'consider the poor' than if the money had been expended in 1s. tickets, whose effect is certainly to create dependence, and not seldom to supply the needs which are the results of idleness and vice?[1]

The number of cases which the District Committees handled was, from the first, surprising, and is in itself proof that the C.O.S. had discovered a need in society and was going a long way towards meeting it. Weekly returns were made to the Council, and monthly summaries were published in *The Times*.

Cases handled by District Committees in 1871[2]

Dismissed:		
Not requiring relief	818	
Ineligible	1,983	
Undeserving	1,150	
Giving false addresses	286	4,237
Referred to		
Poor Law	1,482	
District Agencies	1,101	
Private Persons	770	
Charitable Institutions	556	3,909
Assisted by		
Grants	2,446	
Loans	828	
Employment	295	
Letters to hospitals	358	
Labour Register	433	4,360
Total		12,506

[1] C.O.S. Islington Committee, 12th *Annual Report*, 1882-83, p. 16.
[2] C.O.S., 3rd *Annual Report*, 1871.

District Committees and Practice of Casework

The busiest office was Marylebone, with 1,862 cases, the quietest was Holborn, with 29. In 1872, 15,374 cases were decided; in 1876, 19,173; in 1878, 15,111; in 1879, 21,445. The number of paupers in the Metropolis during these years was falling. In 1871 it had been 142,371 (on the last day of the 4th week of March); in 1878 it was 84,160. The number of paupers per 1,000 of population, 44·2 in 1871, was 23·4 in 1878.[1]

In judging this early casework, the large number, about one-third in 1871, who were not assisted is certainly as important as the number who were helped or referred elsewhere. The category of 'undeserving' cases was a source of difficulty both to friends and critics of the C.O.S. In 1883 the Council attempted to turn criticism aside by explaining that the ineligible and undeserving included those who did not need relief or who had withdrawn their applications, those found to be impostors or guilty of 'such misconduct as makes it impossible to render effectual assistance', those ineligible owing to infirmity or some other cause which made temporary assistance of no permanent advantage, or who could be helped by relatives; and lastly the man whose 'condition is due to improvidence or thriftlessness, and there is no hope of being able to make him independent of charitable or Poor Law assistance in the future'.[2] Misconduct, as many case histories showed, meant drink, habitual laziness and 'vice'.

In this view, the Poor Law existed for two kinds of person, both being in a state of destitution: those whose condition was their own fault, through laziness, improvidence or misconduct, and 'chronic cases of distress, whether caused by illness or by age'. For the sake of the former, relief must be

[1] Local Government Board, 17th *Annual Report*, 1887-88, p. 227.
[2] C.O.S., 15th *Annual Report*, 1883, p. 54.

of a deterrent character; for 'the existence of the Poor Law and the obligation imposed on it of giving necessary relief in all cases is, in spite of all its checks, a strong practical temptation to improvidence'. Abuse of relief could only be checked by 'making it as distasteful as possible to the applicants; that is, by insisting (as a general rule) on a labour test or residence in the workhouse'. But this was manifestly unfair to the other class of poor persons, even if it was argued that they should have shown forethought and saved against evil days (this dilemma confronted all Poor Law administrators as well as outside critics of the system). Hence for the deserving poor charity must come to the rescue, and by pensions or other forms of aid give help to those 'reduced to distress without fault or improvidence of their own, even persons who have not made the best use of their opportunities, but whose previous position and temperament would make the workhouse almost intolerable'.[1]

Some undeserving cases may be cited from the Hammersmith District Committee's report for 1873. A widow had broken her collar-bone in an accident and her son, aged 10, was in danger of losing his situation for want of boots: 'on inquiry it was found that she resorted to a public house every evening, and broke her collar-bone when under the influence of drink'. In another case a woman with four children applied for help, her husband having been out of work for two weeks and the family in great distress; inquiry showed that the husband was very lazy and he and his wife confirmed drunkards. A widow's plea for help was dismissed on the ground that she was a bad character, much given to drink. Two cases were referred to the Poor Law; that of a widow of 76, very feeble, who would be better cared for in the work-

[1] These quotations are from the 2nd *Annual Report*, 1870, pp. 5-6.

C. S. Loch: portrait by Sargent

C. S. Loch as a young man

house; and that of a woman with four children whose husband had deserted her: the case was referred to the Relieving Officer and the husband arrested and sent to prison for three months.

The problem of the undeserving was not merely one of words. As far as words went, the C.O.S. got out of the difficulty by changing 'undeserving' in its tables to 'not likely to benefit' in 1886; by 1888 it had replaced this by the completely non-committal 'not assisted'. The fact remained that the 'unassisted' might be those who most needed help but least deserved it (the 'problem families' of to-day), while those helped, the respectable and the provident, ought least to have needed help. As Helen Witmer has pointed out, the C.O.S. suffered from having two conflicting objects: to make relief efficient (through co-operation and personal service) and to make relief unnecessary (by encouraging thrift and self-support).[1] It did not accept the idea that there would always be some who needed help in society as it then was; at the same time it accepted the Poor Law as the final refuge of the hopeless and the undeserving. Thus the selective charity of the C.O.S. presupposed the bare minimum which the undiscriminating Poor Law must by law provide for the destitute.

It was as well that the C.O.S. accepted these limitations of its work, even if its reasoning was faulty. For it could only do casework if it limited its case load; otherwise it could not, on its own terms, assist anyone properly. For it must always help in order to strengthen character and self-support, never to pauperise; and to do this meant studying the circumstances of each family by the careful taking down of case histories, by inquiry, visiting, correspondence. And this, prying though it sounded, was done, at least when the C.O.S. lived up to its ideal, in the spirit of friendship, of the personal

[1] Helen Witmer, *Social Work* (New York, 1942), p. 143.

service which the better-to-do owed to their poorer neighbours, in the spirit of charity.[1]

In saying this, however, one encounters another set of difficulties in C.O.S. casework. It accepted the existing class-structure and called on persons who could give time or money or both to help the less fortunate. To the present generation this suggests an unpleasantly patronising air; but we may be in danger of reading our own ideas back into a society which was less sensitive about class differences not because they were narrower but because they were wider. We may dislike the element of moral judgment in the C.O.S. categories and decisions. It implied a sternly individualist philosophy, and paid the poor the compliment of assuming they shared it. The C.O.S. constantly talked of character, seeking the cause of poverty in this man and that man, and not in society. But this also was both a virtue and a defect. It limited, even bitterly resisted, the intervention of the State, and prevented the Society (like most people outside it) from seeing the problem of unemployment for what it was; but at the same time the approach to each 'case' as that of a man or woman in need, in circumstances unique to each, seems very modern, the essence of contemporary casework, particularly on the psychiatric side. In fact, as we shall see, the C.O.S. did attempt to apply study, knowledge and the scientific method to discovering and removing the causes of poverty in general; casework and the poverty of individual families was only part of its concern. Nor was it without critics in its own day.

[1] Here as elsewhere in this chapter I am repeating part of what I have written in 'Charity and Casework in Late Victorian London', previously cited (*Social Service Review*, Sept. 1957, reprinted in *Social Work*, 1958). See also Una Cormack's stimulating account in 'Developments in Case-work', *loc. cit.*; Kathleen Woodroofe, 'The Charity Organisation Society and the Origins of Social Casework', *Historical Studies* (Australia and New Zealand), November 1959; and the account in chapter 6 of A.F. Young and E. T. Ashton, *British Social Work in the Nineteenth Century*.

At the same time the C.O.S.'s use of casework was not a static thing. It changed over the years, partly from experience, partly from the pressure of events. At first the 'caseworkers' came from two extremes: the leisured voluntary worker, the man of independent means, the older married woman or spinster, the young unmarried daughter on the one hand, the working-class Agent on the other. The idea of voluntary work, and its identification with an individualist philosophy, hostile to socialism, handicapped the growth of modern, non-partisan, professional casework.[1] Yet the C.O.S. in its next stage (from 1881 onwards) began to employ a salaried staff to supplement the work of the volunteers. In this and in its later provision for training it helped to found the profession of casework.

Of course the C.O.S. did not invent casework[2]: the lawyers did that. Precedents for it, as we have seen, were not lacking. The contribution of the C.O.S. was to develop and refine it and to give it characteristics which it has borne ever since. It is the combination of conditions which the C.O.S. insisted upon which makes its casework important in the history of social work. In the casework of the C.O.S. seven things were combined: district offices, the case paper, the use of a professional staff, the emphasis on the character as well as the circumstances of the applicant, the preservation of the family and family responsibility, the classification of cases, and co-operation between different agencies, both public and voluntary.

The financing of the work of the District Committees was no mean undertaking. In 1873 the Paddington Committee had a balance sheet of £1,165, 1s. 6d., and spent £388, 2s. 8d. on office and other expenses, £332, 0s. 3d. on aid. Marylebone's

---

[1] This point is well made in Kathleen Woodroofe's article cited above.

[2] Young and Ashton, *British Social Work*, p. 113.

balance sheet was £781, 19s. 8d., expenses £372, 15s. 8d., aid £343, 12s. 0d. Hampstead's balance sheet was £246, 12s. 4¾d., and it reported the salary of a 'Charity Officer' as £73, and aid given as £20, 2s. 0d. Bethnal Green's accounts balanced at £140, 18s. 3d., Hackney's at £449, 3s. 9d., North St Pancras and Highgate at £176, 17s. 11d. These were typical figures for the early days.

As the District Committees grew, their relation to the parent body, the Council of the C.O.S., gave rise to disagreement. Members of the District Committees believed that theirs was the real work of the C.O.S., yet it was controlled by the Council and the Society's headquarters. To some extent, the distinction was unreal, since the Council consisted of the chairman and honorary secretaries of the District Committees (who were members *ex officio*) and two representatives elected annually by each District Committee, with the addition of persons elected by the Council, such 'additional members' not exceeding a quarter of the total membership. The federal character of the C.O.S. was thus affirmed. In point of fact, however, the C.O.S. had a life apart from the District Committees, particularly when it possessed an influential secretary, staff, publications and considerable financial resources at its headquarters. The relations of the two parts were a perennial problem.

There were, however, two reasons for the Council claiming some authority over the District Committees. One was financial. The first committees (Marylebone, Kensington, Paddington and St Georges', Hanover Square, all founded in 1869) were all in districts which contained well-to-do families as well as poor families. The ideal of neighbourliness – the obligations of rich to poor – was not here handicapped by geography or finance. But as District Committees were established in poorer areas they found, like the Guardians of the Poor in the same areas, that the greater their need of voluntary workers and of funds, the less their resources. The wealthier committees were urged to help the poorer in both ways, and some of them did so. This was a precarious method. In 1872, therefore, the Council established a District Committee Aid Fund, and henceforth solicited contributions both to this and to its fund for headquarters and general expenses. The District Committees, particularly the wealthier ones, continued to raise as much of their own funds as possible by themselves.

There was a second reason why friction between Council and District Committees was unavoidable. The C.O.S. was founded to preach and apply certain principles of charity; what if District Committees, acting in its name, were untrue to its principles or inefficient in their work? The matter was first discussed by the Council in 1872, and on November 18 a report of a committee was adopted which recommended that districts should be subdivided into divisions, each under the charge of a member responsible for keeping in touch with the other charitable agencies, the relieving officer and the School Board visitors. At the same time an Assistant Organising Secretary (H. Howgrave Graham) was appointed at headquarters to give help to the weaker District Committees (4th Report).

In 1875 the District Committees were again under the scrutiny of the Council. Two members, S. D. Fuller and A. D. Graham, printed and circulated a pamphlet criticising the District Committees for poor office work and organisation, failure to co-operate with other agencies, and a willingness to leave most of the work to their paid Agents (usually one for each committee), some of whom could not even spell.[1] The Council appointed a committee, which in due course presented a 'vigorous and outspoken report'. A permanent

[1] *Charity Organisation Review,* 4: 129 (April 1888) obituary of E. Peters.

Sub-Committee on District Work was appointed, District Committees with a surplus of voluntary helpers were urged to detach some of their members for service in the poorer districts, and it was proposed that the collection of funds should be centralised at headquarters. This last proposal was not carried out, though the District Committee Aid Fund at headquarters continued to be a source of revenue for the poorer District Committees.

APPENDIX

The principles of the work of a District Committee (Extract from the Annual Report of a District Committee, printed as Appendix IV in 8th *Annual Report* of the C.O.S., 1876, pp. 24-5. For the first part of this statement, see above, p. 26).

The working man does not require to be told that temporary sickness is likely now and then to visit his household; that times of slackness will occasionally come; that if he marries early and has a large family, his resources will be taxed to the uttermost; that if he lives long enough, old age will render him more or less incapable of toil – all these are the ordinary contingencies of a labourer's life, and if he is taught that as they arise they will be met by State relief or private charity, he will assuredly make no effort to meet them himself. A spirit of dependence, fatal to all progress, will be engendered in him, he will not concern himself with the causes of his distress, or consider at all how the condition of his class may be improved; the road to idleness and drunkenness will be made easy to him, and it involves no prophesying to say that the last state of a population influenced after such a fashion will certainly be worse than the first. One thing there is which true charity does require the working man to be told, and it is the aim of this Society to tell him, not in words merely, but in acts that cannot be confuted. We desire to tell him that those who are born to easier circumstances sympathise with the severe toil and self-denial which his lot imposes upon him; that many are standing beside him ready and even eager to help if proper occasion should arise; and that if he, or wife, or child should be stricken with *protracted* sickness, or with some special infirmity, such as we all hope to escape, there are those at hand who will gladly minister to his necessities, and do their best at least to mitigate the suffering which it may be beyond their power to remove.

CHAPTER III

The Council and the Repression of Mendicity, 1869-1875

It is difficult to say who or what constituted the C.O.S. at any particular time. When people spoke of the Society they might mean the body of its members and subscribers, or the Council, or the Secretary and the staff at the central office, or the District Committees and their members, voluntary workers, paid staff and offices. To many people, rich and poor, it meant principally the District Committees, and here, as we have seen, lay its practical work and the demonstration of its theories. Yet to the educated lay public the C.O.S. stood for a philosophy of charity, and for a body of people who proclaimed this philosophy in reports, letters, speeches and deputations on a variety of questions.

The task of expounding this philosophy and of applying it to the study of social conditions belonged to the Council. The members of the Council were (1) the chairmen and honorary secretaries of the District Committees, who were members *ex officio*, (2) the two elected representatives of each District Committee, (3) the 'additional members' elected by the Council, up to one quarter of the number of representatives of the District Committees, (4) representatives of other charitable associations. The membership was thus a large one: 73 in 1871, perhaps twice that in 1898, including, besides those in the first two categories, 13 additional members and 11 representatives of Metropolitan charities.[1] The

[1] These last appeared first in 1875, representing the Metropolitan Visiting and Relief Association, the Society for the Relief of Distress,

The Council and the Repression of Mendicity

Council met every two weeks, sometimes every week, at 3 or 4 in the afternoon, except during the summer when meetings were suspended. In 1880 meetings were attended by some 30 members, as a rule, and were devoted to reports of the Administrative Committee and other committees, and to discussions and resolutions on points of policy concerning the Society.

The first chairman of the Council was Lord Lichfield, who held this office until his resignation in 1877. He was the second Earl (1825-92), and succeeded to the title in 1854. His seat was at Shugborough, Staffordshire. He had been Liberal Member of Parliament for Lichfield in 1847-54. Besides his interest in the C.O.S., he worked for the establishment of reformatories. Subsequent chairmen held office for a year, though occasionally longer. They included Prince Leopold (youngest son of Queen Victoria), the Duke of Northumberland, Lord Aberdare, General Sir Orfeur Cavenagh, Hon. Sir Charles Fremantle, Albert Pell, M.P.[1]

Of the other members of the Council in the early days one of the most influential was Sir Charles Trevelyan, the brother-in-law of Macaulay. He had retired after a distinguished career, spent partly in India, where he had been Governor of Madras and finance minister, and partly at home, as assistant secretary to the Treasury. His administration of relief works

the Strangers' Friend Society. The societies represented in 1898 included the first two, and the Jewish Board of Guardians (F. D. Mocatta), the Metropolitan Public Gardens Association, the Metropolitan Association for Befriending Young Servants, the Invalid Children's Aid Association, the Society of St Vincent de Paul, the Metropolitan Provident Medical Association, the London Mendicity Society, the East End Emigration Fund, and the Children's Country Holiday Fund.

[1] Albert Pell (1820-1907), of Hazelbeach, Northants., Conservative M.P. for S. Leics. 1868-85; an advocate of strict administration of the Poor Law, in Brixworth and St George's-in-the-East (Guardian, 1876-89). See his *Reminiscences* (1908), and S. and B. Webb, *English Poor Law History*, II, i, 443.

in Ireland during the Famine, and his share in the reform of conditions of entry and work in the Civil Service in 1853 are well known, his work for charity organisation less so. They were not incompatible. At the Treasury he had shown his passion for hard work, his appetite for information, his readiness to give unasked for (and sometimes tactless) advice. In administering famine relief he had frequently written of the demoralising effects of charity: dependence was a 'moral disease', deaths by starvation 'a discipline'.[1] He was a frequent speaker at meetings of the Council of the C.O.S., and played a large part in its work on casual wards and night refuges, on soup kitchens, provident dispensaries, voting charities, Italian beggar-children in England, and the care and training of mental defectives. He died in 1886.[2]

For the daily administration of the Society's work a smaller body than the Council was clearly necessary. This was the Administrative Committee, which met once a week, and consisted of nine members elected annually by the Council (in 1878 the number was raised to 15). Three members formed a quorum.[3] In addition, there were various standing sub-committees. One on District Work was formed in 1876, and in that year there were three others at work: on Mendicity (later called the Inquiries Committee); on Co-operation; on Finance and Collection. A Medical committee was formed in 1877 as an outgrowth of an earlier special committee which had examined medical charities. In addition, the Council frequently appointed special committees to inquire and report upon particular subjects.

[1] Jenifer Hart, 'Sir Charles Trevelyan at the Treasury', *English Historical Review*, January 1960, vol. 75, p. 99.

[2] See *Dictionary of National Biography* and notice of his death in *Charity Organisation Review*, July 1886.

[3] C.O.S., *By-Laws of the Council*, 1876 and 1887, *C.O. Reporter*, March 14, 1878, p. 53. The Administrative Committee also included three *ex-officio* members (the Treasurer, Chairman and Vice-Chairman of the Council) and 5 co-opted members.

The Council and the Repression of Mendicity

The work of the Council and of the central office was supported by subscriptions and donations. In 1870 these amounted to £659. Total expenditure that year was £1,664, 17s. 3d., of which salaries accounted for £670, 10s. 6d. The deficit was made up by payments from a Guarantee Fund raised by the Marquis of Westminster and other noblemen and gentlemen, which helped to support the work until 1874. By that year income from subscriptions and donations (which numbered about 450) had risen to £3,153, 4s. 10d. Subscriptions to the District Committee Aid Fund totalled £1,285, 5s. 0d. (including grants by six District Committees). The Council's budget for general expenses was £3,653, 3s. 10d. Salaries were the largest item, rent, printing, postage the next largest. The *Reporter* cost £254, 7s. 7d., offset by revenue of £104, 4s. 0d. from its sale. Secretaries' salaries totalled £975, clerks' and inquiry officers' £707, 12s. 3d., the housekeeper's £34, 10s. 4d.

The work of the Central Office at 15 Buckingham Street can be classified under four heads. There was the supervision of the work of the District Committees. There were certain special functions which the Central Office performed, partly because they were less suited to the work of the District Committees. There was the maintenance of a library and the publication of books, pamphlets and a magazine, by which not only the District Committees but also the public at large could be helped and educated on questions of charity and poverty. There was, lastly, the leadership of the movement for charity organisation throughout the country, and, indeed, the world. Here the C.O.S. publications, the Secretary's letters to the press, the holding of meetings, lectures, conferences, all played their part.

Of the special functions discharged by the Central Office, the oldest and longest-lived was that of inquiring into fraudulent charities and exposing, and on occasion prosecuting, promoters of bogus charities and writers of begging letters. In 1882 no less than 2,057 reports were made by the Inquiries section on impostors of one sort or another, in 1883 1,039, in 1885 622, the decline being partly the result of a policy of shifting much of this work to the District Committees.

As early as 1872 the Council prosecuted a Mr Frederick Cox, who called himself honorary secretary of the Free Dormitory Association; his trial was stopped by his absconding. The National Bible and Clothing Society was also prosecuted, and five impostors convicted. In 1877, when Dr Barnardo was charged with making money out of the voluntary orphanages which he had started and which he served in a supposedly honorary capacity, the C.O.S. appointed a committee to go into the matter, but was denied any co-operation by the trustees of the Barnardo Homes and took no part in the prosecution. The charges were referred to a court of arbitration, which eventually exonerated Barnardo; subsequently, the management of his homes was reorganised.[1] In 1887 the C.O.S. won an expensive case against F. G. Helmore, promoter of the bogus Victoria Homes for Waifs and Strays; but it failed to recover its costs since Helmore was a bankrupt. Voluntary Fire Brigades were another target of the C.O.S. Often they lacked any equipment, and their collectors pocketed 40 to 50 per cent. of their takings. Certain men – the names of Samuel Titlow, Henry Brien, Ponsford, Secombe, recur – made a business of promoting these brigades (19th *Annual Report*).

One very large part of the Central Office's work was the building up of its reference library. This still exists, and

---

[1] See two C.O.S. pamphlets, *C.O.S. and the Reynolds-Barnardo Arbitration* (1878), and a circular issued on September 15, 1877; and for a friendly account A. E. Williams, *Barnardo and Stepney* (1943), pp. 110-15.

comprises over 2,000 volumes, most, though by no means all, of the nineteenth and early twentieth centuries. No aspect of poverty and social work is left out: poverty, housing, health, hospitals, public health, unemployment, the Poor Law, crime, prisons and penology, charities and philanthropy, care of the blind, the crippled, the insane and feeble-minded, drink and temperance, child welfare, education, school meals, nutrition, birth control, emigration, savings banks and thrift – all are represented. There are also works on economics and economic history, co-operation, co-partnership, socialism, land reform, small holdings, farm colonies, social insurance. Massive bound volumes of reports and minutes of evidence of royal commissions and select committees, and other government publications, are here also; and, of course, the many publications of the C.O.S. and files of its periodicals. Nowhere was the doctrine of the C.O.S. more faithfully illustrated than in its library: that the many-sided campaign against poverty must be based on intelligence, research, and knowledge of the problems, economic, social and spiritual, which are involved. There must be precise knowledge of the law, of questions of administration, of engineering, of medicine; and of the best theory and practice of the day.

And the knowledge must be disseminated. The C.O.S. took to publication as a duck to water. In those days of cheap and quick printing, the agenda and drafts of reports could as well be put into print as typed – perhaps better. There were also the reports of special C.O.S. committees, and the annual reports of the Society and of the District Committees. The weekly *Charity Organisation Reporter* was started in 1872; it was run at a loss (£277 for the year 1881), and eventually replaced by the monthly *Charity Organisation Review* in 1885. In addition, pamphlets and tracts were produced from the earliest days (some later collected in *Charity Organisation Papers*).

Meanwhile the C.O.S. never forgot the promise of its full title: the Society for Organising Charitable Relief and Repressing Mendicity. If the District Committees gave expression to the first part of the title, the Central Office did to the second. The amount of work the Society did from the very start in investigating the causes of poverty and the methods of relief is extraordinary. Its proposals aimed not only at improving charity but at attacking poverty. The emphasis varied with the times. In the early 'seventies, when many reports were issued during the secretaryship of C. B. P. Bosanquet, it was more concerned with uncovering those kinds of charity which actually encouraged mendicity and demoralised the poor without effectively helping them. In the 'nineties, when the Society was again very active in producing reports under C. S. Loch's secretaryship, the emphasis was rather on the better care of the handicapped, such as invalid children and feeble-minded persons, whose poverty was involuntary.

The methods followed by the C.O.S. to make its views known on particular subjects naturally varied with the circumstances. In many cases it appointed special committees, including men and women of public standing and expert knowledge, most of them not necessarily members of the C.O.S. The report of the committee, after adoption by the Council, might then be the subject of a deputation to the appropriate minister in the government. Public meetings and letters to the press were other methods of propaganda.

Night refuges was one of the first subjects to engage the special attention of the C.O.S. A conference on the subject was held at the C.O.S. offices on June 8, 1870; the Marquess of Westminster, the Earl of Lichfield, Viscount Eliot, Sir Charles Trevelyan and some fourteen other persons were present. Trevelyan spoke at some length: now that all workhouses had casual wards there was no need for night refuges, which only encouraged vagrancy and crime by accepting all comers without inquiry and providing no remedial treatment. A representative of one of the refuges, Mr Gurney Hoare, Treasurer of the Playhouse Yard Refuge (founded 1819) of the Houseless Poor Institution, replied to these charges. A resolution was passed urging night refuges to assume a remedial character, and a committee was appointed to draw up a report under the chairmanship of J. A. Shaw Stewart of the Newport Market Refuge. This recommended that vagrants should be kept out of the refuges and no one admitted without inquiry: and that one of the largest and best endowed should be converted into an adult industrial school.

Many refuges, so the C.O.S. claimed, did turn to C.O.S. principles. In the case of a recalcitrant the Council sent letters to members of the governing committee. The subscribers to another, the Free Dormitory Association, received similar letters, but eventually, as we have noticed earlier, the C.O.S. prosecuted its manager, Mr Cox, who absconded.[1]

Sir Charles Trevelyan's speech at the conference on night refuges deserves to be rescued from oblivion.

The London predatory class pass from casual wards to night refuges, and from one night refuge to another; and the existence of this great proletaire class was in great degree owing to these institutions. These people are in a far better position than persons in the highest ranks of society, for, however high a person may be, he has to defray, out of his income, whatever that may be, his expenses of living, and of meeting the various claims incident to his social position; and what he can spend on pleasure depends upon what is left after all other claims have been satisfied. But

[1] *Conference on Night Refuges* (C.O.S., 1870), containing Report of the Committee on Night Refuges; C.O.S., 2nd, 3rd and 4th *Annual Reports*, 1870-72.

not so this predatory class of people. They had no science, no literature, no devotion to politics – nothing, in short, to divert them from indulgence in the merest sensual and criminal pleasures. They were provided with supper, bed and breakfast free of cost, and they spent their time in going the round of these institutions, where they had leisure . . . to spend their waiting time in devising schemes of crime, the fruits of which were spent in the public-house and brothel.[1]

The C.O.S. tackled the question of 'employment relief' as early as 1871, when Dr Hawksley proposed that parochial workshops should be set up with public funds, but with taskmasters, teachers and tools provided by the C.O.S., to give work for the unemployed. A sub-committee was appointed, including Sir Charles Trevelyan (chairman), Dr Hawksley, Octavia Hill, A. H. Hill, E. W. Hollond, W. M. Wilkinson, Major-General Cavenagh and others. It reported against Dr Hawksley's proposal. Able-bodied destitute persons should be relieved only by the Poor Law, and subject to a labour test in a labour yard or otherwise.[2] Sir Charles Trevelyan insisted that improvement works and relief schemes must be rigidly distinguished, because the former, being popular and likely to be supported by local pressures, confused the question of relief. Improvement schemes, if justified in themselves, should be carried out by men employed on adequate wages; relief work should be confined to the infirm and helpless, and paid for on the lowest scale necessary for subsistence.[3]

Vagrancy and mendicity were attacked by another special committee, which included 49 members of both Houses of

[1] *Conference on Night Refuges*, pp. 9-10.

[2] C.O.S., *Employment*: Report of the Sub-committee (1871).

[3] C.O.S. 27th *Annual Report*, 1895, pp. 20-1. This report compared conditions at the time of the founding of the C.O.S. in 1869 and in 1895.

Parliament and gentlemen qualified to represent 27 English counties. It reported in July 1872, after studying the methods of repressing mendicity used in certain counties. It recommended repression, and constituted itself a permanent committee to carry on the good work.[1] On a similar subject, street-sellers, the C.O.S. sent a memorial to the Home Secretary in 1871.[2]

A form of charity which disturbed the C.O.S. in its earliest existence was the Soup Kitchen. A report was issued in 1871, giving details of 107 'Soup-Kitchens and Dinner-Tables' in London. Some were run as commercial undertakings, though they accepted soup tickets (and were presumably reimbursed by the societies distributing them). One sold soup at 2d. per quart or 1d. per basin, and Melbourne Irish Stew for 2d. a pint. Branches of the Australian Meat Agency offered a penny dinner. Others were philanthropic, though some of them charged a penny, which might simply encourage begging. In any case food was given without inquiry, which helped many who did not need help, and left more money for 'gin-palaces and low public-houses'. In a square mile in the East End there were 165 public-houses and as many beer-houses, taking in £450,000 per year; a school fee of 2d. per child in the same area would only produce £10,053. It was better to make soup kitchens self-supporting, or leave the provision of cheap cooked food to commercial enterprise.[3]

Another subject which attracted the early attention of the C.O.S. was that of Italian children imported by *padroni* to assist in begging or as organ-grinders. A report, which owed

[1] C.O.S., 4th *Annual Report*, 1872.

[2] 3rd *Annual Report*, 1871.

[3] C.O.S. *Report upon the Metropolitan Charities Known as Soup Kitchens and Dinner-Tables*, 1871; C.O.S. report on *Soup Kitchens* in 1877, which stated that their number had greatly diminished.

E

much to Ribton-Turner's work, was issued in 1877 and a deputation sent to the Home Secretary in July; he promised to stop the traffic, and issued instructions for the purpose on August 6.[1]

The treatment of children was of natural and perennial interest. A report listing 23 day nurseries in London and describing 14 of them, prepared by W. G. Howgrave, was issued in 1872.[2] The extension of elementary education to all children raised special problems of C.O.S. doctrine, since any free service to the children might weaken the responsibility of parents and family. In 1872 it offered the services of its District Committees to the Divisional Committees of the London School Board to give information concerning parents who claimed they were unable to pay school fees.

Three years later the C.O.S. was able to put its ideas on helping needy school children to the test. Francis Peek, a member of the London School Board, promised £1,000 a year in 1875 for three years to enable the District Committees of the C.O.S. to give adequate relief to necessitous children referred to them by the Divisional Committees of the School Board. The usual principles of investigation were applied, and the moral was pointed in the 7th *Annual Report* of the C.O.S. (1875): '. . . the results already show that but for the thorough system of investigation adopted by the society, relief might often have been given to undeserving and worthless persons whose earnings, if they had not been wasted through intemperate habits, would have enabled them to provide for the wants of their families'.

In the provision of good houses for the poor the C.O.S. took a keen and fruitful interest, spurred by Octavia Hill's enthusiasm for the twin causes of housing and charity. The

[1] *Italian Children; Report of C.O.S.*, 1877; 9th *Annual Report*, 1877.
[2] *Report on the Crèches or Public Day Nurseries of London, 1872.*

first venture of the C.O.S. into this field was, however, a curious one: an inquiry into Octavia Hill's own initial venture into house-management. The Medical Officer of Health for Marylebone was persuaded to condemn some of her houses as insanitary – an order afterwards withdrawn – and the Council apparently feared that this criticism of the work of a member would reflect on the C.O.S. as a whole. Somewhat to Octavia Hill's distress a sub-committee was appointed on November 20, 1871, to inquire into the sanitary and financial success of her plan for improving the conditions of the poor. The committee inspected some of her houses, and gave them and her a clean bill of health.[1]

Early in 1873 the Council appointed a strong committee to consider means of action for improving the dwellings of the poor of the Metropolis. Lord Napier and Ettrick, who had devoted much attention to questions of public health and public works during his recent term as Governor of Madras, was chairman; the members included Lord Shaftesbury, Lord Lichfield, 5 other peers, 28 members of parliament, 14 representatives of housing companies and societies, 2 representatives of the Association of Medical Officers of Health, and 40 stalwarts of the C.O.S., including Octavia Hill, Sir Charles Trevelyan, C. B. P. Bosanquet. The committee first surveyed the societies which existed for building good dwellings for letting at low rents on which dividends could be paid to investors: the Metropolitan Association for Improved Dwellings of the Industrious Classes, founded in 1841, and the Improved Industrial Dwelling Company Ltd., begun in 1863 under the leadership of Sir Sidney Waterlow, Lord Mayor of London, with a capital of a quarter of a million pounds. The Peabody Trust – founded by an American

---

[1] The report of the sub-committee, adopted by the Council on February 28, 1872, is in the *Reporter* for that date. See also C. E. Maurice, *Octavia Hill*, p. 262.

philanthropist in 1862 – was putting up its blocks of working-men's flats. An immediate ancestor of the C.O.S. committee was a committee appointed by the Society of Arts in 1864, which had published a report on Dwellings for the Labouring Classes in 1865. Nor was legislation lacking: the Artisans' and Labourers' Dwellings Act (the Torrens Act) of 1868 for the demolition of insanitary property, the Labouring Classes' Dwelling-Houses Act of 1866 permitting local authorities to construct houses and to borrow for the purpose, and the Street Improvements Act of 1872 which required the Metropolitan Board of Works to acquire and sell or let land for the building of working-class houses in replacement of those demolished in street improvement schemes. Some cities, such as Edinburgh, Glasgow, Liverpool, had special powers under local improvement acts.

The committee held sixteen meetings, and there were other meetings of sub-committees also. The report found that only 27,000 persons had been housed through the efforts of the housing companies, less than half the annual increase of the metropolitan population. What was needed was much more good housing near to working-men's places of work; building in the suburbs was desirable, but more workmen's trains would be needed, and only seven of the twelve railway companies were then running them at all. New construction in built-up areas was handicapped by the difficulty of acquiring sites for building. Hence the committee recommended that municipalities be given powers of compulsory purchase of land for working-class houses, such land to be resold to companies or societies which would construct the new houses on commercial terms.[1]

Many other persons and agencies were now interested in working-class housing. Its promotion fitted in with the social

[1] *Dwellings of the Poor:* Report of the Dwellings Committee of the C.O.S., 1873.

programme of Disraeli's new government. The C.O.S. Committee's report, on the basis of which the C.O.S. sent a memorial to the Home Secretary, played its part – but how great a part it is hard to say – in bringing about the Cross Act, the Artisans' Dwellings Act of 1875. Octavia Hill's personal influence was certainly important; her work was mentioned in the debate in Parliament on the bill, and passages from one of her articles were read by Sir Ughtred Kay-Shuttleworth (a member of the C.O.S.). Joseph Chamberlain's improvement scheme for Birmingham (the Corporation Street scheme) and Chamberlain's advice were also of importance. The Act gave power to town councils (in London the Metropolitan Board of Works) to make improvement schemes for insanitary areas, to acquire such areas, and to demolish and erect houses thereon (houses so built were subsequently to be sold).

A sequel may well be mentioned here. The Council returned to the subject of housing in 1880, when it appointed a committee (of rather similar composition to that of 1873) to examine the causes of difficulty and delay in carrying out the Artisans' Dwellings Act and other measures. A preliminary report and minutes of evidence [1] were accepted by the Council on November 8, and sent to the Home Secretary with a letter urging the appointment of a Departmental Committee. When, however, the final report was presented on May 2, 1881, it became the subject of controversy in the Council, which voted on June 17, after three meetings on the subject, to omit the report's conclusions and recommendations on the ground that a Select Committee of the House of Commons had meanwhile, and 'partly at the instance of the Council', been appointed. This vote of 8 to 7 so incensed the

[1] C. S. Loch's printed drafts of these, prepared for the consideration of the Council at its meeting of November 8, 1880, are in a volume, 'Dwellings', in the C.O.S. Library.

minority that the matter was brought up again in the Council on August 2, when the Rev. S. A. Barnett moved the adoption of the report (minus the recommendations). The minority produced its own report, identical with the majority's as to its statement of facts, but including the recommendations. The Council decided to 'receive' and circulate both. It was a storm in a teacup. All the members agreed on the slowness and costliness of getting anything done under the Cross Act; the recommendations discounted the usefulness of the Act and pinned their hopes on the gradual movement of working men out of the congested districts, encouraged by more workmen's trains.[1]

The training and care of handicapped persons was the subject of two reports in these early years. On July 13, 1874, the Council created a special committee on the training of the blind, its members being mostly experts on the subject. It held 40 meetings. Its report recommended the earlier education of blind children (from the age of five), partly in company with sighted children; it stressed the need for more teachers of the blind, more grants-in-aid for industrial training, more provision of employment for the blind, improvement in blind workshops, the importance of co-operation among the blind societies of the Metropolis, leading to the establishment of central records and a central depot for the sale of goods. An appendix listed the metropolitan agencies for the blind and blind pension funds, and gave extracts from Acts of Parliament.[2] These, as the Annual Report of the C.O.S. pointed out, enabled the Poor Law authorities to pay the entire cost of educating at charitable institutions blind children and deaf and dumb children, without placing

[1] These reports are in two volumes entitled 'Dwellings', in C.O.S. Library; see also C.O. *Reporter*, August 4, 1881, 'Proceedings of Council'.

[2] *Training of the Blind:* Report of the Special Committee of the C.O.S., 1876.

the parents in the status of paupers and so disenfranchising them.[1]

A similar committee on the education and care of idiots, imbeciles and harmless idiots was appointed on June 21, 1875. Sir Charles Trevelyan was honorary secretary, and the members included several doctors, the Earl of Devon, Lord Lichfield, Sir J. P. Kay-Shuttleworth, U. J. Kay-Shuttleworth, Lieutenant-General Cavenagh, Albert Pell. It held 13 meetings, visited 4 institutions, and obtained information on practice in the British Colonies, the United States and other countries. Its main recommendation was that a distinction be made between dangerous lunatics and the harmless – the term feeble-minded soon replaced idiots and imbeciles in common usage. The harmless could be trained by proper methods, and many could undertake useful work; for this purpose they should be separated from the dangerous lunatics (and from paupers in the workhouses) and placed in special institutions. Voluntary bodies could not provide for the numbers involved (about 49,000 of all ages in England and Wales in 1871), and the action of the State was necessary. The Metropolitan Asylums Board had already established three special institutions; the counties should follow suit, combining where necessary to build asylums housing 2000 adults and 500 juveniles. The relief given for persons of this sort should not (and in fact did not) put their families in the status of disenfranchised paupers; but the families should contribute to their support within their ability. The State should also give support to voluntary asylums which would admit harmless lunatics from lower middle class and upper-artisan class families at suitable rates.[2]

[1] C.O.S. 7th *Annual Report*, citing 4 & 5 William IV, c. 76, s. 56.

[2] *Education and Care of Idiots, Imbeciles and Harmless Lunatics: Report of Special Committee*, 1877.

The Charity Organisation Society

A large deputation, including Lord Shaftesbury, presented this report to the President of the Local Government Board on May 16, 1877. His reply was favourable, and a clause distinguishing the harmless lunatics from the others, and empowering the counties to provide schools and asylums for the former, was included in the County Government bill – which, however, was later withdrawn.[1] Action was not taken until 1889, when the Royal Commission on the Blind, the Deaf and Dumb, under the chairmanship of Lord Egerton of Tatton, issued its report. It proposed that education should be compulsory for blind and deaf and dumb children, and that for them, and for imbeciles and for feeble-minded children, special provision should be made by the school authorities.[2] These recommendations were carried out by legislation in 1893 as far as blind and deaf children were concerned by the Elementary Education (Blind and Deaf Children) Act.

Another subject which for long interested the C.O.S. was the working of medical charities and the London hospitals. The sub-committee drew up a code of rules for Provident Dispensaries, and summoned a conference of governors and medical officers of hospitals on December 12, 1871, to promote the transformation of free dispensaries and out-patient departments into provident dispensaries.[3] The next step, so the 5th *Annual Report* (1874) announced, was to get hospitals to investigate the circumstances of persons attending their out-patient departments. The Royal Free Hospital permitted such an inquiry in 1874; the result showed the 49 per cent. of those giving correct addresses would have

[1] C.O.S. 9th and 10th *Annual Reports*.

[2] *Report of the Royal Commission on the Blind, the Deaf and Dumb, etc., of the United Kingdom.* C. 5781, 1889.

[3] 1st *Report of Medical Committee of the C.O.S. with Rules for Provident Dispensaries:* adopted by Council, October 30, 1871; C.O.S., 2nd and 3rd *Annual Reports*.

been able to contribute to a provident fund had one existed.[1] Thereafter progress lagged, until in 1877 the committee was enlarged under a new chairman, Timothy Holmes. This succeeded in launching, in 1879, the Metropolitan Provident Dispensaries Association, a body independent of the C.O.S. and devoted to providing medical benefits on a provident basis to working people. Sir Charles Trevelyan played a large part in its founding.[2]

How far did the C.O.S. succeed in some of its other objectives: charity reform, co-operation between charitable societies? A defect of many charitable societies was that they were 'voting charities'. Subscribers received a certain number of votes by which poor persons in need could be nominated to receive help from the society. This led to an unfortunate and often heartbreaking canvassing for 'letters' (for more than one vote might be needed) by the person needing help; the houses of well-to-do people had to be visited, entailing long journeys on foot and the resolution to overcome the rudeness of servants and the interrogation or supercilliousness of the philanthropist whose help was sought. Even then, applicants might be voted on in a meeting of the society, in which 'elections' were sometimes contested. Esther Waters' efforts, which were successful, to get a letter admitting her to a hospital for her confinement, are sympathetically described in George Moore's novel, and remind us of this unnecessary obstacle to the operation of charity.

Sir Charles Trevelyan moved the Council to take a stand against the system in 1872, and a meeting of representatives of voting charities was called by the Lord Mayor in 1873. The C.O.S. position was, of course, that elections were undesirable since what was needed was the careful investigation

[1] 5th and 6th *Annual Reports*.
[2] 9th and 11th *Annual Reports*.

of all persons who applied for help. Resolutions and a paper were sent to the principal voluntary societies. For this early action the C.O.S. encountered a good deal of criticism – the beginning of its persistent unpopularity. It was charged with wanting to get the patronage of the charitable societies into its own hands.[1] The system of voting charities gradually died away.

In another direction, promoting the co-operation of charitable bodies, whether through the District Committees or through the work of the Council, the C.O.S. had little or no success. Even the attempt to amalgamate the C.O.S. and the Mendicity Society, whose objects were complementary, came to nothing after negotiations, begun in 1872, had dragged on for some years.

[1] C.O.S., 5th *Annual Report*; Helen Bosanquet, *Social Work in London*, pp. 370-4.

CHAPTER IV

C. S. Loch and the 'Church of Charity'

In 1875 a new era began for the C.O.S. with the appointment of a new secretary, Charles Stewart Loch, who held office until 1913. Before long Loch and the C.O.S. were almost interchangeable terms, and his long years of service made him the embodiment of the C.O.S. idea for friend and foe alike. To him more than anyone else must be ascribed the idea of charity which the C.O.S. elaborated, and to which it strove to convert the country, for over a generation.

Charles Stewart Loch was born on September 4, 1849, in Bhagulpoor, Bengal, where his father, George Loch, was Collector in the East India Company's service. George Loch was later Judge of the High Court of India from its creation in 1862 until his retirement in 1872. The Lochs came of a professional family in Edinburgh which had prospered in a modest way and had at one time had as its seat the house of Drylaw, an attractive eighteenth-century mansion still standing in the western suburbs of the city, not far from Granton.[1] Loch's mother, Louisa Gordon (daughter of a major in the Bombay Engineers), died when he was born, and he was brought up in England by Mr and Mrs Bell, old friends of the family in India. He was educated with

[1] On the Loch family see Gordon Loch, *The Family of Loch* (privately printed, Edinburgh, 1934). Henry Brougham Loch, 1st Baron Loch of Drylaw, Governor of the Cape and High Commissioner in South Africa, 1889-95, was a first cousin once removed of C. S. Loch.

his elder brother at Glenalmond, and in 1869 entered Balliol College, Oxford, just before Jowett's mastership began in 1870. He read Classical Moderations and History, and for a time had T. H. Green as his tutor. He also studied drawing under Ruskin, the Slade Professor. He formed lasting friendships with several members of a remarkable generation: Bernard Bosanquet, A. C. Bradley, C. B. Heberden, A. L. Smith, F. H. Peters (later Fellow of University College, Oxford). Poor health (he was asthmatic), from which he suffered intermittently throughout his life, hampered his Oxford career, and he did not graduate till 1873. Rejecting thoughts of entering the Church, he began work as a Clerk at the Royal College of Surgeons in London.[1]

At this time Loch took up voluntary work for the C.O.S., serving the Islington District Committee as a member of the executive committee in 1874, and as honorary secretary in 1875. His friendship with his future wife, Sophia Emma Peters, daughter of Edward Peters (a member of the Council of the C.O.S.) and sister of F. H. Peters, influenced his thoughts in the same direction, since Miss Peters was at this time serving as secretary to Octavia Hill. When he was asked by C. B. P. Bosanquet, half-brother of his friend Bernard Bosanquet, whether he would let his name be proposed for the Secretaryship of the C.O.S., he was 'taken aback' but agreed,[2] and was subsequently chosen, in November 1875. The Council's only doubts were on the score of his youth, a handicap which, Lord Lichfield remarked, he was likely to outgrow.

[1] There is an article on Loch by R. B. Mowat (his son-in-law) in the *Dictionary of National Biography, Supplement, 1922-30.* I am indebted to my mother for additional information. See also the article by Kathleen Woodroofe, 'C. S. Loch', *Social Service Review*, 31: 400-13, December 1958.

[2] Letter from Loch to S. E. Peters, October 29, 1875 (in possession of Mrs R. B. Mowat).

C. S. Loch and the 'Church of Charity'

Loch's influence in the C.O.S. derived from his forcefulness as an administrator and as a formulator of ideas. He was a man of great determination, as Sargent's portrait of him in the Committee Room of the C.O.S. suggests. A secretary is always in a strategic position; he prepares the agenda of meetings and writes up the minutes. On the many special committees of the Council in the early days Loch was also secretary. None was more skilled than he in drafting reports and framing possible resolutions; and copies of his drafts, printed and marked 'private and confidential', show how his marshalling of business helped to determine the Council's action.[1]

By degrees, his writings and speeches, his letters to *The Times* as secretary of the C.O.S., made Loch a public figure. He was a contributor to the *Economic Journal*, a member of the Council of the Royal Statistical Society in 1899 and winner of the Society's Guy Medal for his paper on 'Poor Relief in Scotland'; he was Tooke Professor of Economic Science and Statistics in King's College, London, from 1904 to 1908. He was a member of the Royal Commissions on the Aged Poor (1893-95), the Feeble-Minded (1904-08) and on the Poor Laws (1905-09). He was well known abroad. He gave a paper at the Congrès International d'Assistance at Paris in July 1889. In 1896 he visited the United States to attend the National Conference of Charities and Correction at Grand Rapids; he also visited New York, Philadelphia, Baltimore, Washington, Boston and Chicago. He was knighted after his retirement.

To his family and friends Loch showed other sides of his character. The Lochs lived in Bedford Park, that early and still attractive example of a garden suburb in Chiswick, and

[1] See for example the copy of the interim report on Housing (1880), and drafts of a letter and statement to be sent to the Home Secretary, in a bound volume, 'Dwellings', in C.O.S. library; also two letters printed in the appendix to this chapter.

were part of a cultivated society which included the Yeats (parents of W. B. Yeats), Goddard Orpens, Todhunters, Gielguds, Leightons, Hills, Hindleys, Nashs, Synges, Unwins, Yorke Powells, Cockerells, Pagets, Pinero, Coventry Patmore, Lucien Pissaro. Loch was a member of a local club, the Calumets, which met on Sunday evenings for discussion; he was one of the founders of Chiswick High School, a successful but short-lived co-educational venture. Later, the Lochs moved to Oxshott, in Surrey, where they were neighbours of the Bernard Bosanquets; and later still they settled at Little Bookham, Surrey.

Like so many of his generation, Loch was a man of varied interests. His sketch-books, and some of his letters from summer holidays in Switzerland, are adorned with delicate little sketches and water-colours: heads of men and women seen in the market-place in Algiers, a waterfall, a distant mountain. His letters are full of precise observation of flowers, birds, fossils, and lively descriptions of scenery and of fellow-travellers. At home, he was a keen gardener, and a lover of walking. He was fond of music, and had a fine singing voice.

He was a great reader, especially of poetry; Wordsworth he was particularly fond of. In the evening he always read aloud to his wife: Browning, Meredith, Scott, Thackeray, Dickens, Jane Austen, George Eliot, Kipling, Sheridan, Goldsmith, the *Iliad* and the *Odyssey* were among their favourites. Much of his reading was professional: Poor Law reports, Bonar's life of Malthus, Dowell's History of taxation, for example. He never gave up reading the Greek and Latin poets. In his diary he complained of 'very few books read' in the year 1881, and then gave a formidable list: Browning ('often'), Chaucer, Mallory's King Arthur; de Musset's plays; *Felix Holt, Theophrastus*, and articles on George Eliot; Froude on Carlyle, a book on Cobden, Morley on Compromise, a life of George Sand; 'and three books of the Iliad is all the classics I have done, except a few bits of Catullus'.

He was not an orthodox churchman, but might be described as a natural Christian, preferring to give his two children lay sermons on Sunday rather than regular attendance at church. His poems show his belief in a God of Love, present in everything, and in the immortality of the soul; and he had a sturdy conviction in progress and the improvement of mankind.

> *So may I live two lives, one outward fair,*
> *One inward spirit-fed, a living prayer.*
> 'The Two Lives', 1880.

> *Then to my soul doth from the mountains call*
> *A poet's voice, 'God lives, God lives in all'.*
> 'The Master', 1887.

These poems came from a volume, *Things Within*, printed for the author in 1922, and containing poems written by Loch between 1872 and 1912. Not all are serious. It contains ballads he wrote on holidays. 'The Downs of Aberdovey' and 'The Maiden of Linn Cai'; 'Of Rex, my Dog'; 'A School Song' (written for Chiswick High School), and a prologue written for a performance in Bedford Park of 'Rumpelstiltskin', a children's play, written by Miranda Hill, Octavia's sister.[1]

Loch's influence was paramount in shaping the ideals of the C.O.S. and in expounding them in addresses and articles. He wrote much: in the *Charity Organisation Review* and in other C.O.S. publications; and the Annual Reports of the Society were his work. True, his authorship must in many

[1] C. S. Loch, *Things Within* (Oxford: Blackwell. Printed for the Author, 1922).

cases be inferred. There are three major expressions of his thought: his book *Charity Organisation*, published in 1890, a reprint of his paper given in Paris in July 1889; his long article for the 10th edition of the *Encyclopaedia Britannica* (1903) on 'Charity and Charities', reprinted and expanded in *Charity and Social Life* (1910); and the posthumous collection of some of his addresses, *A Great Ideal and its Champion* (1923). Perhaps the best statement of his faith, in which he refers to 'a church of charity', is in his paper on 'The Development of Charity Organisation' (1903) (extracts from which are printed in the Appendix to this chapter).

Loch accepted and elaborated the analysis of poverty and charity which the C.O.S. had followed from its foundation. Poverty is principally the result of a moral failure, and indiscriminate charity contributes to or aggravates the failure. The Poor Law, unless very strictly administered, is a natural target for his criticism: 'it serves as a bounty on dependence and is a permanent obstacle to thrift and self-reliance.'[1] In the 18th *Annual Report* of the C.O.S., for 1886, he wrote a long essay on pauperism and its causes. Pauperism 'is not a poverty of possessions, but a poverty and degradation of life, an habitual reliance on others, due to want of self-control and foresight, and of the goodness that underlies these things. The man who, in this sense, is a pauper has lost some of his manhood, and will not, or cannot, do a man's work in the world: and the woman has lost some of the influence of her womanhood in the home and in the family.'[2] The drift into this sort of pauperism is encouraged by charities which give free breakfasts or coal or money, easing the path of those who prefer to live by casual labour and their wives' earnings; it is encouraged by the proselytising charity of the Churches, which sets the poor to praising ''igh

[1] *Encyclopaedia Britannica*, 11th ed., V, 885.
[2] C.O.S., 18th *Annual Report*, 1886, p. 2.

C. S. Loch and the 'Church of Charity'

Church and chicken broth'. Pauperism may, he admits, have other causes: weakness of character or vice; sickness, poor health, lack of work and incompetence; inability to make provision against old age. But character is the important thing. 'To prevent distress charity has for its further object to preserve and develop the manhood and womanhood of individuals and their self-maintenance in and through the family. . . . By self-maintenance is meant self-support throughout life in its ordinary contingencies – sickness, widowhood, old age, etc.'[1]

This insistence on self-support and condemnation of many forms of relief derived partly from Loch's analysis of the 'economics of charity'. Wages can be adequate if properly spent (for example, through abstinence from alcohol). To supplement low wages is to prevent wages from rising: even a postponed supplementation, old age pensions, will have the same effect by discouraging thrift. 'Only necessity schools most men, especially the weak, to whom it makes the most difference ultimately, whether they are thrifty or whether or not they save for the future in any way.[2]'

In addition, however, Loch had been much impressed, as his *Encyclopaedia Britannica* article shows, by his view of the part played by public charity in the decline of the Roman Empire. Under the *lex Clodia* (58 B.C.) the Roman citizen became entitled to the *annona civica*, the regular free allotment of bread, pork and oil as his share in the former *ager publicus*. Thus arose a 'degraded pauperism' in which the hardworking few maintained a swarm of idlers. 'There could hardly be a more effective method of degrading his manhood and denaturalising his family. He was also a voter, and the alms appealed to his weakness and indolence; and the fear of displeasing him and losing his vote kept him, socially, master

[1] *Encyclopaedia Britannica*, 11th ed., V, 885-6.
[2] *Ibid.*, p. 886.

F

of the situation, to his own ruin. If in England now relief was given to able-bodied persons who retained their votes, this evil would also attach to it.'[1] There was another reason also for insisting on a self-supporting citizenry. With the growth of democracy no one was outside the pale of citizenship. 'Pauperism is the social enemy of the modern State. The State wants citizens. It cannot afford to have any outcast or excluded classes, citizens that are not citizens.'[2]

This individualist philosophy is, not unnaturally, combined with a strong distaste for any sort of socialism. Criticising Charles Booth's scheme for old age pensions in 1892 as involving a transference of £12 millions annually from rich to poor he wrote: 'We have yet to learn that a transfer of this kind does not ruin and pauperise the receivers. Only those who adopt a socialist view of society and hope that the State instead of private individuals will become the general fund-holder would find such a reform satisfactory; to them it would be a stepping-stone to a completer division.'[3] In the *Encyclopaedia Britannica* article he included a section on 'Charity and Socialism', in which he contrasts the interventionism of charity (by transforming the individual) with the aim of 'recasting society itself on a new economic plan, as does socialism. . . . To charity this position seems to exclude the ethical element in life and to treat the people primarily or chiefly as human animals. It also seems to exclude the motives for energy and endeavour that come from self-maintenance.'[4]

The rigour of this doctrine was mitigated by other parts of Loch's thought. He believed, with Chalmers, that society

[1] *Encyclopaedia Britannica*, 11th ed., V, p. 867.
[2] *Charity Organisation*, p. 4.
[3] 'Pauperism and Old-Age Pensions', a paper read to the Poor Law Conference for the South Wales District, May 1892, Bernard Bosanquet (ed.), *Aspects of the Social Problem* (1895), pp. 158-9.
[4] *Encylopaedia Britannica*, 11th ed., V, 886.

C. S. Loch and the 'Church of Charity'

was an organism, and that the family, strengthened by and strengthening the community, was the fundamental unit. Charity is the means by which family and society are preserved. Charity 'has sought to transform the world by the transformation of the will and the inward life in the individual and in society. It would intensify the spirit and feeling of membership in society and would aim at improving social conditions as science makes clear what the lines of reform should be.'[1] This it does by offering friendship, kindness: χάρις and ἀγάπη, the charity of kindness and goodness, rather than ἐλεημοσύνη, alms-giving under a sense of religious obligation. Charity is 'love working through the individual and the social life'.[2] Charity 'is an elemental force in social life. . . . It has within it the fervency of religion, and endowed with a purpose and discipline it is a source of common good.'[3] The C.O.S. 'should be a Great Companionship of Charity, West with East, rich with poor, the elder with the younger generation'.[4]

Charity must, however, work with knowledge. 'It requires a social discipline; it works through sympathy; it depends on science. . . . Its first thought is to understand, and to treat with the reverence that comes of understanding, the growing and expanding elements out of which Society is formed – the individual and the family, the groups of members within the community and the community itself.'[5] Charity is 'a science, based on social principles and observation. Not to give alms but to keep alive the saving health of the family becomes its problem. . . .'[6] Loch could thus

[1] *Ibid.*
[2] 'If citizens be friends' and in *A Great Ideal and its Champion*, p. 19.   [3] *Ibid.*, p. 90.
[4] C.O.S., 17th *Annual Report*, 1885, p. 8.
[5] *A Great Ideal*, p. 19.
[6] *Encyclopaedia Britannica*, 11th ed., V, 885. See also a statement of his creed in 1903 in the appendix to this chapter.

claim to be an early sociologist, and it was no accident that the first school for the training of social workers, which he and the C.O.S. founded (though they did not continue to control it), was called the School of Sociology.

An interesting analogy may be drawn between Loch's views and those of his friend Bernard Bosanquet, the philosopher and in later years a member of the Council of the C.O.S. In Bosanquet's *Philosophical Theory of the State*, first published in 1899 and dedicated to Loch, will be found a sort of right-wing Hegelianism which justified Loch's views of man and the state and the science of sociology. 'Society and the State. . . have their value in the human capacities which they are the means of realising'[1]; 'the end of the State is moral purpose'[2]; 'the ultimate end of Society and the State as of the individual is the realisation of the best life'.[3] The best life can, however, 'only be realised in consciousness', and the amount the State can do to advance it is limited, since it can only 'secure the performance of external actions'. The State may hinder hindrances to the good life, but positive action will only have beneficial results if the individual will is ready to respond. 'The promotion of morality by force . . . is an absolute self-contradiction. . . . We ought, as a rule, when we propose action involving compulsion, to be able to show a definite tendency to growth, or a definite reserve of capacity, which is frustrated by a known impediment. . . .'[4]

The bearing of this theoretical position upon policies of State intervention for the improvement of the individual, such as the C.O.S. opposed, is clear enough. State action to secure better houses or wages, or to provide schools, will accomplish nothing unless the material facts are 'charged with mind and will'. Putting a family into a good house will

[1] B. Bosanquet, *Philosophical Theory of the State* (4th ed., 1923), p. 310.
[2] p. 188.   [3] p. 169.   [4] pp. 169-79.

C. S. Loch and the 'Church of Charity'

not of itself provide 'an element in the best life . . . unless there was a better life struggling to utter itself, and the deadlift of interference just removed an obstacle which bound it down . . .'.[1] With charity Bosanquet was not (in this book) concerned. He minimises class since it is no longer a political institution, and condemns the idea of 'the poor' as a class marked by the function of dependence, 'as a permanent object of compassion and self-sacrifice'.[2] 'Socialism', he observes, 'at its best, unites with recent political economy and with those who try to "organise" or rationalise charity, in challenging the preconception that poverty must be recognised as a permanent class-function.'[3]

* * * * *

Much of Loch's best and most lasting work was done in several of the special reports which the C.O.S. published during his secretaryship. In these not only his mastery of the facts but a certain flair for showmanship are made plain. The reports had a semi-official air about them. It can hardly have been an accident that the C.O.S. printer for many years was Spottiswoode & Co., who did much of the government's printing. Some reports looked not unlike Blue Books, with bluish covers and an official-looking title page. The members of the special committee were set out in formal fashion. At the bottom of the list we find C. S. Loch, Secretary; and perhaps also the statement, at which we raise our eyebrows a little, 'Mr R. Hedley, in attendance on behalf of the Local Government Board'. There follows a table of contents and the recommendations of the committee. After this came the Minutes of Evidence, headed each day by the entry: Present, Mr Bousfield in the Chair, followed by the names of the members present. Mr So-and-So, examined, is the next

---

[1] *Ibid.*, pp. 184-5. [2] pp. 294-5. [3] p. 296.

entry; and the questions put to the witness, numbered as in a Royal Commission's inquiry, and his answers, are recorded verbatim.

The report on the 'Homeless Poor of London' (1891) is an excellent example. A special committee of the C.O.S. re-examined the old subject of night refuges and casual wards. Its report runs to nearly 200 pages, of which 150 are the evidence and index. It includes the evidence of 26 persons, superintendents of refuges, the police, two 'casuals', Poor Law Officers. London's homeless night population on a typical winter night is estimated at 938 persons in refuges (including 193 women and 33 children) and 877 in casual wards (including 129 women and 10 children); in addition there were the inmates of common lodging-houses and Salvation Army shelters, not all of whom were necessarily homeless. Both the numbers and the accommodation for them had declined since 1870; casual ward accommodation by one-third, that of night refuges by nearly a half. The report recommended the conversion of some refuges into small homes for the treatment of the homeless, increased powers of detention for the clients of the casual wards under conditions 'somewhat less favourable' than those the regular inmates of the workhouses enjoyed, and the formation of a Central Council representing the night refuges and the Poor Law to promote co-operation between all the authorities concerned.[1]

An earlier but lengthier study was of another old question, free school meals, which was linked with the early interest of the C.O.S. in soup kitchens and meal tables. A special committee was appointed in 1887 on Soup Kitchens, Children's Breakfasts and Dinners and Cheap Food Supply. Its report, *Charity and Food*, argued that to supply cheap, clean food

[1] *The Homeless Poor of London:* Report of a Special Committee of the C.O.S., June 1891.

at commercial prices was a public service; to supply it free or below cost without inquiry into the needs and means of its recipients was a false and dangerous charity. To do this for school children was no better. It weakened the duty of the family and encouraged the mother in lazy habits since, if the children got a good meal at school, she might give up cooking at home and feed them on scraps, using the money saved for bad purposes; moreover, supervision of meals encroached upon teachers' leisure, and the provision of facilities for cooking and serving (even if the food was provided by voluntary societies) was a misuse of rates levied for educational purposes.[1] *The Better Way of Assisting School Children* (1893) was to give sympathetic help, after inquiry, to deserving families whose children were in need, and to prosecute or force upon the Poor Law those who were negligent, improvident or worthless. This was to follow the individual method as opposed to the general method of charity. These recommendations were buttressed by numerous case histories, the result of inquiries into the families of needy children in certain schools, and an examination of the causes of distress (illness, widowhood, drink or vice, 'alleged want of work, usually combined with laziness', insufficient savings, neglect of relations).[2]

Loch gave much thought to the treatment of the handicapped: cripples, epileptics and the feeble-minded. In 1891 the C.O.S. appointed a committee under the chairmanship of Timothy Holmes, F.R.S., F.R.C.S., President of the Royal Medical and Chirurgical Society, Consulting Surgeon to St George's Hospital: Holmes was also Chairman of the Council of the C.O.S. The committee included several doctors,

[1] C.O.S., 21st *Annual Report*, 1890.

[2] *The Better Way of Assisting School Children* (Charity Organisation Series; 1893), which also summarises *Charity and Food* and the first report of the Special Committee to consider the best means of dealing with school children alleged to be in want of food (1891).

representatives of homes and asylums, Boards of Guardians and Voluntary Societies. It presented an interim report, with tables of statistics, to the Council on July 27, 1891; resolutions were also submitted to the International Conference on Hygiene and Demography, and a strong deputation waited upon the President of the Local Government Board on March 29, 1892.[1] From the work of this committee came two books, published by the C.O.S., in the Charity Organisation series and written largely by Loch. *The Feeble-Minded Child and Adult* (1893) described the causes and characteristics of feeble-mindedness and discussed methods of training – for which no special schools existed then in England. It proposed that the School Boards provide special schools and that where maintenance was also needed the School Boards should provide it also; as it was, it was the Guardians' responsibility, but help given was not, as with the blind and deaf and dumb, exempt from the stigma of pauperisation, though the book suggested that it ought to be. Feeble-minded adults should be provided for in homes supported by voluntary contributions and by payments from the Guardians. *The Epileptic and Crippled Child and Adult* (1893) was similar in scope and spirit. It stressed the need for special schools and homes; no such schools existed in England, and the only two homes were at Maghull, founded in 1889, and one recently started by Lady Heath in connection with the Girls' Friendly Society. The recommendations of the C.O.S. committee were largely repeated in the Report of the Departmental Committee on Defective and Epileptic Children in 1898.[2] In 1899 the Elementary Education (Defective Children) Act permitted the education authorities to provide schools for mentally defective and

[1] The interim report is referred to in *Charity Organisation Review*, September 1891 and April 1892.
[2] C. 8746, 1898.

epileptic children, and made attendance at such schools compulsory.

In 1904 the government appointed the Royal Commission on the Care and Control of the Feeble-Minded, of which Loch was a member. Its report was issued in 1908.[1] It recommended that the protection and supervision of all mentally defective persons should be entrusted to a single Board of Control; and that provision for the maintenance and education or training of mental defectives should be the responsibility of the counties and county boroughs. By the Mental Deficiency Act of 1913 these recommendations were partially given effect; but lunatics remained subject to the Lunacy Commissioners, and education and training remained the responsibility of the local education authority. Defectives were defined as including idiots, imbeciles, the feeble-minded and the moral imbeciles.

What has always been regarded as one of the C.O.S.'s best achievements, and one of Loch's most imaginative ideas, was the introduction of hospital almoners. Loch first expounded this idea to the House of Lords' committee and elaborated it in an article on 'The Confusion of Medical Charities' in the *Nineteenth Century* for August 1892. He was pursuing his familiar theme, prominent in his thought about school meals: one must inquire into all the causes of a person's need; 'medical charity must act in alliance with general charity. Their cause is one.' There must be co-operation between the various agencies. 'What more glaring picture of charitable impotence is there than that destitute persons should constantly apply to a free dispensary for drugs which cannot benefit them if they lack the necessary food?' The name for the new type of social worker he proposed, almoner, he took from that applied to admission

[1] *Royal Commission on the Care and Control of the Feeble-Minded,* v. 8, *Report,* Cd. 4202, 1908.

officers at St Bartholomew's Hospital in the Middle Ages.[1]

The first hospital almoner, Miss Mary Stewart, was appointed at the Royal Free Hospital from October 1, 1895, her salary being paid half by the Hospital and half by the C.O.S. with the help of funds contributed by F. D. Mocatta and S. A. Thompson Yates.[2] Actually, Miss Stewart had been working in the out-patient department of the Royal Free Hospital, on an experimental basis, in the previous winter (i.e. since early in the year 1895); her reports led to the introduction of the more permanent arrangement.[3]

Another subject close to Loch's heart was the reorganisation and better use of the old endowed charities, preferably in association with the voluntary societies. He thus regretted that the reorganisation of London's endowed charities, carried out in 1890, made no provision for this association, and also omitted any provision for the annual review of the new schemes in the light of changing needs.[4] The report of the Royal Commission on the City of London Parochial Charities (1880) led to legislation in 1883 which obliged the Charity Commissioners to frame a scheme applying the City's parochial charities to the service of the Metropolis. Much of the funds were devoted to the purchase of open spaces and the support of polytechnic schools and of libraries.

A greater failure, from Loch's point of view, befell the plans for the co-ordination of London's hospitals and

[1] *The Hospital Almoner* (London 1935), pp. 35-6, whence come the quotations just given.

[2] C.O.S., 40th *Annual Report* (1908), pp. 26-7.

[3] C.O.S., 26th *Annual Report*, 1894 (presented April 3, 1895), p. 23; *C.O. Review*, July 1895, p. 328 (report of Council meeting, June 10, 1895, at which Miss Stewart's appointment was discussed and agreed to).

[4] C.O.S., 21st *Annual Report*, 1889.

C. S. Loch and the 'Church of Charity

dispensaries. In 1889 the Council of the C.O.S., in a *Memorandum on the Medical Charities of the Metropolis*, presented a petition to the House of Lords praying for the appointment of a select committee of inquiry, pointing in justification to the financial difficulties of the voluntary hospitals and the overlapping services of the hospitals, Poor Law Infirmaries, free provident dispensaries and outpatient departments.[1] The petition was supported by the *Lancet* and the *British Medical Journal* and some 1,600 doctors. A select committee was appointed in 1890 by the House of Lords. This committee received from the C.O.S. in 1892 the proposal for a Central Board for London, and gave it its guarded support.[2] Nothing came of it then, but it was revived in 1896, when a large committee of doctors was formed in its favour. The 28th *Annual Report* of the C.O.S. expressed the hope that the formation of the Prince of Wales's Hospital Fund in alliance with the Hospitals Sunday Fund would help to forward the Central Board; but in fact it never came to fruition.

Another reform which the C.O.S. urged – and itself practised – under Loch's leadership was the proper auditing of the accounts of voluntary societies. The Council called a special meeting on the subject in December 1888, at which a paper was read by Mr Gerard van de Linde, member of a leading firm of accountants and auditor of St George's Hospital. Following this, a special committee prepared a report which the Council accepted and published in 1890.[3]

[1] *Memorandum on the Medical Charities of the Metropolis*, C.O.S., 1889, which contains particulars of the finances and administration of the London hospitals.

[2] Select Committee of the House of Lords, Third Report on *Metropolitan Hospitals*, etc., 1892, p. cv.

[3] 20th *Annual Report: Audit of Accounts of Charitable Institutions*, C.O.S., 1888; Report of Special Committee of the C.O.S. on the *Preparation and Audit of the Accounts of Charitable Institutions*, 1890.

APPENDIX

I. Extracts from two letters from C. S. Loch to his wife concerning the Housing sub-committee of the C.O.S. in 1880 (letters in possession of Mrs R. B. Mowat).

October 29, 1880.

... I am going to the Dwellings Committee. Please God I shall hold a bridle on my tongue and get things pushed through – though I feel the unpleasantness of working against a party of people who form themselves into a party on all questions. And Sir U. K. S. [Shuttleworth] with his threat of secession if we don't do what he wants, is really too bad.

Oct. 30, 1880.

... The 'Dwellings' went off all right. I got out a careful agenda raising the exact issue – got it read first and acknowledged to be a fair statement of the point at issue. And it was decided to have a departmental Committee to (inquire) into the Administration of the Acts only – our Committee continuing its work irrespective of it and Sir U. K. S.

II. Extract from a paper by C. S. Loch read before the Council of the C.O.S., June 1, 1903, *The Development of Charity Organisation*: 'Private and Confidential. For Members of the District Committees of the C.O.S.' In bound volume, 'Pamphlets. C. S. Loch', in C.O.S. library.

If I were asked why I joined the Society I should answer that through its work and growth I hoped that some day there would be formed a large association of persons drawn from all churches and all classes who, disagreeing in much, would find in charity a common purpose and a new unity.

C. S. Loch and the 'Church of Charity'

That, it seemed to me, was 'worth anything'. Such an organisation, I thought, could do more than Parliament, or preaching, or books, or pamphleteering. . . . Such an organisation might bring to bear on the removal and prevention of evils a combined force that would far exceed in weight and influence any yet existing. It could make legislation effective, could see that it was enforced. Apart from all legislative interference and with the use of means and influences more far-reaching it could renew and discipline the life of the people by a nobler, more devoted, more scientific religious charity. It could turn to account all that newer knowledge would bring to the help of charity. It could eventually provide out of all classes and sects a great army of friendly and by degrees well-trained workers. It could help us to realise in society the religion of charity without the sectarianism of charity. It would open to many a new path for the exercise of personal influence – influence with the churches, the Guardians, the Friendly Societies, the residents of a district, and 'the common people'. Differing in much, many might unite in this.

This, this hope that there might be what I have sometimes called a church of charity, undeclared it might be and invisible, but in a very real sense actual – a peacemaking, unifying body – has been constantly in my mind.

CHAPTER V

The C.O.S. at the Zenith, 1875-1903: the Start of a Profession

At the end of the nineteenth century the C.O.S. was an impressive body: influential in the public life of the country, busy in its District Committees throughout London, the leader of the charity organisation movement throughout the world. Its Patron was the Queen, its President the Archbishop of Canterbury; its Vice-Presidents, headed by H.R.H. The Princess Louise, the Marchioness of Lorne (later Duchess of Argyle), included two dukes, two marquesses, four earls, four other peers, six bishops, and twenty other persons, among them Octavia Hill, Ruskin, Canon Barnett, C. B. P. Bosanquet, Alsager Hay Hill and H. G. Willink. The Council was equally impressive. Sir Joshua Fitch was chairman in 1898, Lord Methuen in 1899. F. J. S. Edgcombe and Thomas Mackay were vice-chairmen. The 'additional members' in 1898, 13 in all, included Bernard Bosanquet and his wife, Helen Bosanquet, Sir William Chance, Sir William Bousfield, the Earl of Stamford. The Administrative Committee consisted of 19 members: W. A. Bailward (chairman of the Bethnal Green Board of Guardians) was chairman.

We can get some idea of the C.O.S., as a child of its time, from the sort of people, members of the leisured and professional classes, who were active in it. Unfortunately it is very difficult to find out anything about many of them, since their lives, whether quiet or busy, were not such as to gain a place for them in the *Dictionary of National Biography* or any

The C.O.S. at the Zenith

other hall of fame. This is not true of Bernard Bosanquet, Loch's contemporary and friend, professor of moral philosophy at St Andrews for a few years, who joined the Administrative Committee in 1890. Apart from his philosophical work he wrote and spoke frequently about charity. He contributed many of the essays (for example, on 'The Duties of Citizenship', 'Character and Social Causation', 'The Principle of Private Property') in the volume which he edited in 1895, *Aspects of the Social Problem*. His wife, Helen Dendy, whom he married in 1895, was also a prolific writer on social questions. She first appears in the C.O.S. as the (paid) District Secretary for Shoreditch in 1890; after her marriage she was an active member of the Council and the Administrative Committee and for a time was editor of the *Charity Organisation Review*.[1]

Other prominent members included William Grey, Lord Stamford (1850-1910), who succeeded his uncle in the title in 1890. He joined the C.O.S. as a member of the Stepney District Committee in 1885; he was chairman of the Council in 1896. He was also an almoner of the Society for the Relief of Distress, a member of the Limehouse Sanitary Aid Committee, and a supporter of Oxford House, Bethnal Green.[2] Sir Joshua Fitch (1824-1903) had been Principal of Borough Road Training College, and was later Inspector of Training Colleges for Women in England and Wales.[3] Sir William Bousfield (1824-1910) served the C.O.S. in the Kensington District Committee, and was chairman of the Council in 1894-96. His obituary in the *Charity Organisation Review* (April 1910) referred to his devotion to public service as being characteristic of the best of the leisured class, and

---

[1] See Helen Bosanquet, *Bernard Bosanquet* (1924).

[2] *William, Earl of Stamford* (privately printed, 1922); *Charity Organisation Review*, June 1910.

[3] A. L. Lilley, *Sir Joshua Fitch* (1906).

mentioned his work in the hospital out-patient departments, the Metropolitan Provident Medical Association, the Girls' Public Day School Trust. He was chairman of the Clothworkers' Company. Sir William Chance succeeded in 1902 to the baronetcy of his father, head of the family's glass manufacturing firm in Birmingham. He was for many years secretary, and later chairman, of the Central Poor Law Conferences and wrote books on the Poor Law.[1] He was a Guardian of the Poor in Farnham.

Three other men, unknown to fame but prominent in the Society for many years, deserve mention as being typical of the class in society from which it drew its strength. Edward Peters had retired early from the Indian Civil Service on a pension, and had tried running a school and a farm before settling in Chelsea, where he served as a member of the Board of Guardians. He was an almoner of the Society for the Relief of Distress, honorary secretary of the Stepney District Committee, and from 1881 to 1885 chairman of the Administrative Committee of the C.O.S. He had a large part in the reorganisation of the work of the District Committees in 1875. He died in 1888.[2] F. J. S. Edgcombe was another Guardian member of the C.O.S., being a member of the Kensington Board of Guardians for over thirty-five years and chairman for twenty years. He was an active member of the Council, and honorary secretary of the Kensington District Committee from 1871 to his death, which occurred in 1909 when he was 78.[3]

The third was Thomas Mackay (1849-1912). He was born in Edinburgh, the son of a colonel in the East India Company's service, and was educated at Glenalmond and New College, Oxford. He was called to the bar in 1874, but

[1] *Poor Law Conferences*, 1910-11, pp. ix-xix.
[2] *Obituary in Charity Organisation Review*, April 1888.
[3] *Ibid.*, May 1909.

his prospective father-in-law, a Canon of York, doubted his ability to support a wife as a young barrister, and advised him to enter some business to secure a certain income. He went into partnership with a wine merchant, a cousin of his father's, but retired from this after ten years (in 1885). Thereafter he 'devoted his life to the study of social and economic questions and literary work', as a member of the C.O.S. and as a writer and speaker on the Poor Law and charity. He was honorary secretary of the St George's-in-the-East District Committee for twenty-five years, and a vice-chairman of the Council for eleven years. His works – all sternly individualist in tone – included volume 3 in completion of Sir George Nicholls' *History of the English Poor Law* (1899), *The English Poor* (1889), *A Plea for Liberty* (1891), *Methods of Social Reform* (1896), *The State and Charity* (1898), *The Public Relief of the Poor* (1901).[1]

A man of similar station who served for a time on the C.O.S. staff was A. Dunn Gardner, who died in 1902 at the age of 51. He had been called to the bar, but 'decided to forego his chances of worldly success and devote his life to the interests of others'. He was the son of a 'fairly wealthy gentleman', of Chatteris and 37 Grosvenor Place. He was a Justice of the Peace at the time of his death, had served for ten years on the Chelsea Board of Guardians and was described as having no great physical powers.[2] He was honorary secretary of the Society for the Relief of Distress.

By the end of the century the staff of the Central Office had grown considerably. After Ribton-Turner retired when his post of organising secretary was abolished in 1877, Loch carried on alone for a time, but after 1879 there were usually two, sometimes three assistant secretaries. In 1883 E. C.

[1] *Ibid.*, April 1912.
[2] *West London Press*, August 2, 1902 (cutting in C.O.S. library).

The Charity Organisation Society

Price began his long service as assistant secretary; a 'jovial little man' who married a fellow C.O.S. worker rather late in life. He retired at the end of 1930.[1] Of the other, more transient, assistant secretaries the only one known to fame was C. E. Mallett, who served in 1887.[2] In addition there were the members of the staff of a lower grade, the accountant, clerks and inquiry officers – a total of 8 in 1897. They were not listed among the Society's officers in the *Annual Reports*; in the office they were addressed as 'Mr' rather than by surname only.

Finances had kept pace with the growth of the establishment. In 1887 subscriptions and donations had risen to £7,455, 1s. 6d., from about 1,450 persons. A further £1,092, 6s. 0d. was received by the Council for its Relief fund, and £108, 7s. 0d. for the District Committee fund; £524, 19s. 7d. for a fund for obtaining surgical appliances, £2,977, 3s. 8d. for convalescent cases, £1,353, 7s. 9d. for special cases, £1,065, 7s. 2d. for the Emigration fund. The Council's budget for general expenses was £7,605, 6s. 4d., but this included £3,855, 4s. 1d., spent for the work of the District Committees, in grants and secretaries' salaries. Publications (the *Charities' Register* and the *Charity Organisation Review*) cost £555, 12s. 2d., and brought in £299. The Secretary's salary was £600, the Assistant Secretary's £250; the Accountant was paid £183, 15s. 0d., the Inquiry Officer £110, two shorthand clerks £145 and £130 respectively, and two clerks £80 each.

The *Annual Report's* summary of expenditure was as follows:

---

[1] Recollections of Mrs R. B. Mowat.

[2] Sir Charles Mallett (1862-1947), Liberal M.P., 1906-10, Secretary for Indian students at the India Office, 1912-16; knighted 1917, Chairman of the Council of the C.O.S., 1928-31, author of *A History of the University of Oxford* (1924) and other works.

The C.O.S. at the Zenith

1887

	Organisation	Relief
Council	£4,661 12 6	£3,985 17 11
District Committees	£10,391 9 10	£22,261 4 6

In the presentation of these accounts the C.O.S. followed the prescription it offered constantly to its District Committees and to all charitable bodies, that of having a systematic annual audit. The auditors in 1872, and over the years – this was still true in 1913 – were two members of H.M. Exchequer and Audit Department: another suggestion of the semi-official status which the C.O.S. seemed to assume.

Ten years later, in 1897, subscriptions and donations to the Council were £8,620, 0s. 6d. There were six other funds, but only two were of much size: £1,087, 12s. 8d. for convalescent cases, £2,886, 0s. 8d. for special cases. The expenses of the Central Office were £4,484, 1s. 6d. Salaries included £800 for the Secretary, £350 and £200 for two Assistant Secretaries, £253, 15s. 0d. for the Accountant, £185 each for two shorthand writers, £140 for the general clerk, £100 for the copying clerk, £69, 15s. 10d. for the junior clerk, £130 for the Inquiry Officer and £82, 0s. 1d. for a temporary inquiry officer. Grants to District Committees totalled £4,438, 6s. 7d., of which £2,385, 2s. 2d. was for district secretaries' salaries.[1]

By the 'nineties the Council consisted of perhaps 150 persons, including the chairman, honorary secretaries and representatives of the District Committees, the representatives of Metropolitan charities (11 in 1898), and the 'additional members'. Its meetings had perforce taken on a rather more public character than in earlier years. In 1895, for example, 11 special and 16 ordinary meetings of the

[1] C.O.S. 29th *Annual Report*, 1897, pp. 65-73.

Council were held. The former were reported as 'very largely' attended, the figures of 200, 155, 104 being mentioned; the latter had an average attendance of 40, including visitors. Discussion of the Society's business (e.g. finance, appointment of district secretaries) occupied some of the ordinary meetings, but both they and the special meetings were usually taken up with papers, discussions and resolutions on matters of public policy: the unemployed, pauperism, wages and prices, a central hospital board for London, socialist propaganda, collecting savings banks, mentally defective and epileptic children. Several of the papers were by Loch. All meetings were fully reported in the *Reporter* or the *Charity Organisation Review*.

Much of the work of the Central Office was now being done by standing sub-committees of the Council, and it was here, in the 1880's that the C.O.S. made several hopeful attempts to 'organise' charity. For example, in 1879 the Council appointed a special committee to examine the placing of sick persons in convalescent homes – a problem arising from the pressure of applications at certain times of the year. Following the committee's report[1] the Council in 1880 created a Convalescent Homes Committee as a sort of clearing house: 36 homes were to report their vacancies to the Committee; the District Committees of the C.O.S. were to recommend suitable patients; and the Convalescent Homes Committee would allocate the patients to the vacant places.[2]

The Medical sub-committee continued its work of furthering provident dispensaries and co-operation between the dispensaries and the hospitals. Its secretary from 1884 onwards for many years was Colonel Montefiore, R.A. In 1885 it

[1] For its report, see *C. O. Reporter*, April 15, 1880.
[2] *Organisation of Convalescent Aid* (1st Annual Report of the Convalescent Committee of the C.O.S., 1884).

The C.O.S. at the Zenith

undertook the task of supplying surgical apparatus to patients referred to it by the District Committees and inspected by a surgeon. The object was to undermine the method followed by most of the Surgical Aid Societies of helping only those who came with sufficient 'letters' from subscribers to the society. With this development it was natural that the Medical and Convalescent sub-committees should be combined in 1887.

In 1880 another special committee investigated children's homes. It recommended a system of classification, co-operation between the homes and the Poor Law authorities, and a better distribution of cases among the various types of institution.[1] More fruitful was a scheme for visiting and helping invalid children in their homes, proposed by Mr Allen D. Graham and Colonel Montefiore in June 1886, and adopted as part of the Society's work in December. It was financed for a year by Mr Graham. Cases were notified to Colonel Montefiore, as secretary of the Medical and Convalescent Committee, by the hospitals and by him referred to the appropriate District Committees. In June 1888 the Council decided that the scheme had best be separated from the C.O.S., and a friendly parting took place: Graham founded the Invalid Children's Aid Association to carry on the work.[2]

A committee on Emigration was formed in May 1886. Its task was to assist deserving families to emigrate, after their circumstances had been investigated by a District Committee. Lieutenant Haigh, R.N., was its secretary. In 1886 it assisted 21 families and 19 single men to emigrate, at a cost of £523, 4s. 7d. In 1887, its first full year, it helped 155 'cases' or 436 persons; 107 persons went to Canada, 4 to South Africa, the rest to Australia. The average cost was

[1] C.O.S., 12th *Annual Report*, 1880.
[2] *Charity Organisation Review*, II (1886), pp. 265, 305; III (1887), p. 28; IV (1888), pp. 363-6.

· 89 ·

The Charity Organisation Society

£5, 2s. 3d. per person. In 1890 the co-operation of the East End Emigration Fund was obtained and the secretary's salary and services were shared; Lieutenant Haigh's services were terminated and W. Barratt succeeded him. Forty-six cases (138 persons) were assisted, of whom 15 persons went to the United States, 61 to Canada, 7 to South Africa, the rest to Australia. In 1891 the number of persons helped rose to 178, in 1892 to 211, in 1893 to 337; but by 1895 the number had fallen to 130 (43 cases).

A short-lived effort to promote another form of co-operation among London charitable societies deserves mention. This was a Combined Collection plan, similar to that employed in Liverpool. It was started in 1883 and had been joined by 11 societies by 1885. Total collections were £2,478 in 1883-84 and £3,203 in 1884-85 (17th *Annual Report*). Evidently the plan did not take on with the great majority of the charitable societies; for after a brief reference in the 19th *Annual Report* (1888) that it was being slowly developed it is heard of no more.

Meanwhile the zeal of the C.O.S. as a publisher was increasing. The *Charity Organisation Review*, a monthly, replaced the *Reporter* in 1885. Pamphlets and tracts appeared frequently, many of them being republished in *C.O.S. Occasional Papers*, of which four series were issued between 1896 and 1913. These were designed *orbi et urbi*. More ambitious, and more obviously designed to spread C.O.S. ideas and information among the general public, were the books in the Charity Organisation Series, published by Swan Sonnenschein for the Society and edited by C. S. Loch; this began in 1892. Last but by no means least was the great *Annual Charities Register and Digest*, which was first published in 1882 and still appears. *How to Help Cases of Distress*, the introduction to the *Register* written by Loch and growing in length with each edition, was first published separately in 1883 and often reissued; its present-day successor is the annual *Guide to the Social Services*.

These publications, and especially the *Charity Organisation Review*, made the C.O.S. a leader in the charity organisation movement, which grew rapidly in the 1870's and 1880's, not only in the British Isles but also in the United States, the British colonies overseas, and continental Europe. In fact, since the basic ideas of the C.O.S. – visiting, inquiring, co-operation, anti-mendicity measures – had long existed both in London and outside it, the spread of the movement, once there was a vocal body in London to make its ideas known, was to be expected. As early as January 17, 1870, the Council authorised the Honorary Secretary to answer communications from the country, to supply inquirers with the Society's papers, and to solicit the support of local 'persons of influence'. Representatives of anti-mendicity societies attended a conference summoned by the C.O.S. on March 24, 1871; a committee was inevitably formed, and the Council instructed Ribton-Turner to issue papers giving advice to societies being formed in the country on C.O.S. lines. Soon such societies were asking to affiliate with the C.O.S., and a conference was summoned to meet on March 22, 1872, to decide upon the conditions for affiliation.[1] By the end of 1872 eight societies in the provinces had been formed or reorganised on C.O.S. lines and had been granted affiliation: in Birkenhead, Brighton, Chester, Eton, Oxford, Reigate, Winchester, Kingston. At the same time the Council was in correspondence with several other societies in England and Scotland, and with some in the United States.[2]

It was apparently at this time that the C.O.S. issued a series of 'County Papers'. No. 1 was entitled *Suggestions on the best Method of Organising Local Charity Associations with Offices*,

[1] C.O.S., 3rd *Annual Report*.
[2] 4th *Annual Report*.

The Charity Organisation Society

as contemplated by the *Society for the Organising of Charitable Relief and Repressing Mendicity*. It contained a price-list of appropriate stationery which embryo societies could obtain from the C.O.S.: printed invitations to a public meeting, handbills announcing the meeting, preliminary circulars, envelopes for subscribers, sheets of tickets (numbered and unnumbered), placards and handbills, all of which could be bought in lots of 500 or 1,000; they had blank spaces which could be filled in with the appropriate local names and particulars. Another leaflet, *Conditions of Affiliation for Country Societies desiring to co-operate with the London Society*, reproduced the main principles of the C.O.S., which affiliating societies must accept, and added the requirement of sending quarterly returns, and particulars of migratory impostors, to the London Office.

By 1875, 12 provincial societies were affiliated with the C.O.S., by 1879, 18. In that year the *Annual Report* included a list of societies in the British Isles with which the C.O.S. was in correspondence. There were 91 (including the 18 affiliates) distributed as follows:

In towns in England and Wales	73
County mendicity societies (Dorset, Hereford, Kent)	3
In Scotland	9
In Ireland (1 in Belfast, 4 in Dublin)	5
In Guernsey	1

Their names varied greatly: some were charity organisation societies or associations, others were mendicity societies, district visiting societies, associations for improving the condition of the poor (in Scotland). The list of societies continued to grow with the years; the number affiliated with the C.O.S. was 25 in 1893, after which this category disappeared from the list.

As the movement took on this national character attempts were made to establish more systematic and personal contacts between the parts. The Council in London summoned a conference of representatives of provincial societies to meet on May 5, 1881, in Exeter Hall. A paper by Mr W. Moggridge, editor of *Social Notes*, on 'London and Provincial Aspects of Charity Organisation' was read and discussed.

A more ambitious undertaking which continued for many years was the annual conference of charity organisation societies, held at different provincial cities in turn. The first took place at Oxford in October 1890. It was followed by one in London in May 1893, and after this they took place every year in the spring, meeting in such places as Rochdale, Cheltenham, Leicester, Glasgow, Clifton, Belfast. The Leicester conference, held on May 4-6, 1896, was attended by 106 persons: 62 representing 32 provincial societies and 44 representing the C.O.S. in London and 22 of its District Committees. In 1896 there was also held the first district conference of charity organisation societies at Worcester.

To keep the London C.O.S. and the provincial societies in touch the Council formed the Provincial Sub-committee in March 1892. Its very active honorary secretary for many years (until 1908) was N. Masterman, who lived in Dorking. Much correspondence was carried on; provincial societies were visited by representatives from London, sometimes Masterman or someone else, sometimes by a 'regular embassy'; and the provincial societies were encouraged to send visitors to the C.O.S. office in London. In 1895 the C.O.S. published a separate *Register* of such societies; and this included excerpts from the annual reports of many of them.

Brotherly feelings for charity organisation societies abroad also appeared early. In the United States a Society for the Prevention of Pauperism had been founded in New York in 1817, and a similar society took shape in Boston in 1835: district visiting was a feature of both. In 1843 the movement began in New York which within the next thirty years produced about a dozen Associations for Improving the Condition of the Poor in the larger cities; but the A.I.C.P. movement stumbled over one of its chief aims, the promotion of co-operation between existing charitable societies, and the various associations failed or assumed different forms and purposes.

The depression of 1873 produced the first true C.O.S. in the United States, the Germantown Relief Society; its leaders were Samuel Emlin, editor of a local newspaper, and a Unitarian minister, Charles Gordon Ames, who had read of the work of Chalmers and Octavia Hill. Buffalo was the first city of any size with a city-wide C.O.S. The Buffalo Charity Organisation Society was founded in 1877 by an English clergyman familiar with the C.O.S. in London who had emigrated to Buffalo, the Rev. S. H. Gurteen. The society had district committees and offices and a body of friendly visitors; Gurteen published a *Handbook of Charity Organisation* in 1882. Similar societies followed in New Haven, Philadelphia, Syracuse, Newport (Rhode Island), Brooklyn, Indianapolis, Detroit, Cincinnati, Baltimore, Washington; all these were in existence by 1881. The most influential of them all, the New York C.O.S., was founded in 1882. In 1883 there were 25 charity organisation societies scattered through the East and the Middle West, varying widely in form and method. The New York society was perhaps closest in spirit to the London society, though it, like the other American societies, followed ideas and principles of native inspiration. A drawing in its 31st annual report showed the five steps leading up to the door of self-support – a

The C.O.S. at the Zenith

sympathetic hearing, emergency relief, a confidential inquiry, a correct diagnosis, effective treatment.[1]

The first mention of correspondence between the London C.O.S. and American societies occurs in the 4th *Annual Report* (for 1872). In the 14th *Annual Report*, for 1882, a List of Foreign Charity Organisation Societies and Other Societies in Correspondence with the London Charity Organisation Society appears for the first time. Societies are listed in Australia, Austria, Barbados, Belgium, Canada, Denmark, Egypt, France, Germany, Greece, Holland, India, Italy, Natal, New Zealand, Russia, Spain, Sweden, Norway, Turkey and the United States. The total number was 125, of which 29 were in Germany, 19 in France, 18 in the United States, 10 in Austria-Hungary. By 1895 the number listed in the United States was 125.

By the end of the century charity organisation had achieved international stature. Loch's paper for the Congrès International d'Assistance in Paris, and his visit to the United States, are evidence of this. At the annual Charity Organisation Conference of the C.O.S. in 1900 which was held in London, at the Clothworkers' Hall, several overseas visitors were in attendance, and special honour was given to two: R. Treat Paine, President of the Associated Charities of Boston, and R. W. de Forest, President of the New York Charity Organisation Society.

The casework of the District Committees had kept pace with the expanding activities of the Central Office. In 1887 the number of cases was 25,533, varying between 1,828 at St George's, Hanover Square, and 101 at Clapham. Of 8,840 persons denied help, 1,308 were deemed not to need it,

---

[1] This account is based on F. D. Watson, *The Charity Organisation Movement in the United States* (New York, 1922). See also Mary E. Rich, *A Belief in People: A History of Family Social Work* (New York, 1956).

3,905 as not likely to benefit, 242 had relatives able to give help, and 3,385 were left to the Poor Law. The following table portrays the experience of the next decade, when the number of cases declined in the prosperous 1890's:

Paupers in the Metropolis, and number of cases handled by C.O.S. District Committees

	Indoor	Outdoor	Total
1887	58,225	45,505	103,730
1893	60,334	32,733	93,067
1897	65,660	37,458	103,118

Paupers (excl. lunatics and vagrants) on last day of 4th week of March.[1]

	Total	Withdrawn	Not Assisted	Assisted
1887	25,533	2,678	8,840	14,289
1893	24,472	2,666	11,260	10,501
1897	17,814	2,021	8,269	7,524

Cases in C.O.S. District Offices.[2]

The financial standing of the District Committees in 1887 was very much what it had been in 1873. A well-to-do committee such as Kensington had a budget of £1,669, 4s. 6d.; St George's, Hanover Square, and Westminster balanced its general account at £969, 3s. 7d., and its relief account at £1,193, 19s. 3½d.; the corresponding figures for Marylebone were £635, 15s. 4d., and £1,429, 6s. 5d. A committee of intermediate character had £285, 13s. 11d. in its general account and £582, 19s. 2d. in its relief account (St Pancras South). In the East End, St George's East had a relief account of £1,069, 14s. 1½d. and a general account of

[1] L.G.B., 27th *Annual Report*, 1897-98, p. 347.

[2] C.O.S., *Annual Reports*.

The C.O.S. at the Zenith

£230, 6s. 7d. – fairly typical figures. The smallest committee was Eltham, whose total budget was £25, 13s. 1d.[1]

Altogether, in 1887, the District Committees' funds totalled £26,257, 4s. 6d. The Committees collected £7,834, 6s. 11d. in subscriptions and donations and received another £3,176, 2s. 9d. from the Council and £15,246, 14s. 1d. for 'special cases'. The Council's subventions went only to the poorer committees, and provided some of them with almost all the funds of their general account (for office expenses and salaries) and considerable aid to their relief funds. Poplar and South Bromley received the greatest help from this source: the Council contributed £81, 8s. 0d. to its general account (£206, 16s. 3d.), and £344, 18s. 8d. to its relief fund of £1, 414, 2s. 8d. On the other hand the wealthier committees – Kensington, Hampstead, the City of London – contributed to the Council's funds and gave also to one or two of their fellow District Committees.

By 1897 the District Committees' funds had risen to £38,805, of which £1,881 consisted of grants from the Council and £14,986 of funds for pensions. Expenditures in that year totalled £8,970 for office expenses and salaries, £1,692 in general grants, £15,147 in pensions, £2,524 for convalescent cases, £788 for surgical cases, and £9,734 for 'other cases'.

The large sum spent on pensions marked a development of C.O.S. work. Pensions for old people had begun in a small way in the 'eighties: 'there is a continual increase of the Society's work in this direction', the 15th *Annual Report* (for 1883) recorded. By 1885 several District Committees were reporting on their pensions: 50 had been arranged for by St James's, Soho, 74 by Marylebone. In East London the Tower Hamlets Pension Committee was at work. The 20th

[1] Figures from Annual Reports of the respective District Committees; these do not agree with the summary figures given in the table on p. 106, 19th *Annual Report* of C.O.S., 1887.

The Charity Organisation Society

Annual Report, for 1888, described a change in the regulations contained in the Society's 'Manual' which stated that 'where individuals or special charities are willing to take charge of them, the committees are ready to send them the names of persons ascertained to be deserving'. Now the statement was altered to read: 'the Committees cannot undertake to find the pensions which chronic cases need, but will endeavour to procure them from existing charities or from private persons'. In 1890 there were 684 pensions in force, in 1893 915, totalling £9,574, in 1895 1,089, totalling £12,329.

The Society was able to reconcile the giving of pensions with its principles. People ought to avoid dependence in old age by 'good administration' and forethought, and the C.O.S. had no intention of aiding those whose want was due to 'vice, drink and thriftlessness', who must be left to the Poor Law. Rather, it would help those who had done what they could to provide for themselves, and had friends and relatives ready to give help. As the Marylebone Committee put it in 1893:

> It must be understood that the recipients are as far as possible the 'cream' of the old working people of the district. It is plainly impractical to pension every old man or woman whose sole qualification is that he or she has never been seen the worse for drink. The whole value and meaning of the plan would be imperilled, and the true interests of the class it is intended to benefit in so far damaged, were not some standard of thrift and uprightness, family duty and the like, steadily maintained.[1]

The Society's method, in pension cases, was, of course, first careful investigation of the person and the circumstances. Character and evidence of thrift were considered.

[1] 24th *Annual Report*, 1893, pp. 29-30.

The C.O.S. at the Zenith

Past employers, relatives and friends were appealed to. If a sufficient sum or promises for a small weekly pension were not obtained from these sources, money from the Committee's funds might be used to supplement it. Frequently cases were advertised in the *Charity Organisation Review* and individual donors were found. A 'Golden Book' of donors to whom 'heavy' cases might sometimes be referred was kept at the Central Office. In many cases the money did not pass through the Committee's hands at all: thus the total value of the pensions arranged by the Committees was much larger than the sums which each reported that it spent on pensions. The pension was usually taken round weekly by a visitor, thus retaining the friendliness and personal touch between the better-to-do and the poor which was an essential part of the Society's work. 'Voluntary almoners pay the weekly allowances at the pensioners' homes, and thus have frequent and regular opportunities of cheering the old people with a friendly chat, and of reporting to us any change of health or circumstances which may call for special treatment', as the Stepney Committee put it.[1]

A few of the advertisements in the *Charity Organisation Review* in 1895 and 1896 will demonstrate the Society's methods and the type of old people whom it helped (such appeals were, of course, made also for other kinds of people: e.g. to maintain a youth in a colony for epileptics, to board out in the country two little children whose mother was in an asylum).

16,789. The Bethnal Green Committee asks for £3, 5s. towards a weekly allowance to a most respectable widow, aged 71. Her husband had worked for one employer for 35 years, and was a member of two clubs. Her landlord

---

[1] 27th *Annual Report*, 1895, p. 9: a very useful account of the Society's work in pensions, pp. 8-15.

lets her have a good room at a low rent, as she has been his tenant for so many years. The Committee think therefore, that she belongs to a class which should not be dealt with by the Poor Law, and wish to supplement the allowance made by two private donors.

17,111. The Shoreditch Committee ask for £9, 2s. towards continuing an allowance to a carpenter permanently disabled by asthma. He had saved a considerable sum by small savings, on which he lived for three years; while able to work he allowed his mother 5s. a week. Clergy and visitors contribute, and baker allows bread gratis.

17,692. The St Olaves' Committee ask for £2, 9s. to enable them to complete a pension of 7s. a week to an old lady of 85. The remainder is given by a former employer, and by clergy.

18,266. The Holborn Committee appeal for £2, 1s. 6d. to complete a pension of 10s. weekly, for six months, for a very deserving old couple. They were formerly in a much better position (farmers), but have fallen into great poverty through no fault of their own. Grandchildren and a daughter give 6s. weekly, and provide a room for them rent free.

18,111. The Holborn, Clerkenwell and St Lukes' Committee ask for £7, 16s. for six months to complete a pension of 10s. 6d. for a thoroughly respectable old couple who have done their best to provide for old age. Twenty years ago the man had a position in the city at 19s. weekly. In 14 years they managed to save £30. They invested a legacy of £100 in the Liberator Building Society, and lost nearly all. The man belonged to Foresters' Club for 30 years, but the Court to which he belonged broke four years ago. An only son gives 1s. weekly and a mission 3s. 6d.

The C.O.S. at the Zenith

Thus did the C.O.S. respond to the movement for old age pensions. Why then, in its own words, its 'unswerving opposition to means of helping the aged by grants from the State'? Because they would defeat the ends of charity.

Charity, rightly understood, strengthens social obligations . . . but grants without charity weaken them. And only such grants can be made by the State. It has no power of considering the needs of the individual. . . . It can endeavour to encourage thrift. . . . But it cannot foster it as the outgrowth of the character of the man and his family – cultivated, therefore in such a way as will strengthen his responsibility, and to such a degree as will in general suffice to meet all his needs. Lastly, charity considers the family; State grants ignore it.[1]

It was in the daily work of the District Committees that the voluntary workers were most prominent, both on the committees, as helpers in the office, as visitors to the homes of the poor. Two must serve as representative of a great host. Margaret Gladstone, daughter of Professor J. H. Gladstone, F.R.S., and future wife of Ramsay MacDonald, did C.O.S. visiting in Hoxton, where she was also a school manager and secretary of the District Nursing Association, in the early 'nineties.[2] Susan Grosvenor, daughter of the Hon. Norman Grosvenor, a son of Lord Ebury, worked in the Marylebone District Office in Baker Street before her marriage (in 1907) to John Buchan (later Lord Tweedsmuir).[3]

An important change, which altered the rôle of the volunteer, was now coming over the social work of the C.O.S. It was becoming, by the end of the century, a profession, marked by the appearance of salaried workers and

[1] 27th *Annual Report*, 1895, p. 15.
[2] J. Ramsay MacDonald, *Margaret Ethel MacDonald* (1912; 6th ed., 1929), pp. 87-8.
[3] Lady Tweedsmuir, *The Lilac and the Rose* (1952), p. 90.

the development of training. Of the new class of secretaries (*not* honorary secretaries) of District Committees it might be said that it was an outgrowth of the Inquiry Agents of the earliest days – who, indeed, continued to be employed. But there were important differences. The secretaries were on salaries and came from a higher social class than the Agents. And they were undertaking not only casework but organisation and training. The work of the District Office had outgrown purely voluntary methods and staffing; a professional cadre must be called into being.

Though the first paid secretary was appointed in 1875[1] the new beginning really dates from 1881. A report to the Council, after several District Committees had been visited to study their work, stated that the Committees, though they usually bestowed much care on their casework, had no means 'for interesting new adherents or for organising charity'. In February, a special conference of hon. secretaries and delegates of District Committees was held, and a resolution was passed (and subsequently adopted by the Council) that Committees should be immediately strengthened, 'if possible, by voluntary help; if not, by well-paid superior officers'.[2] In conformity with this resolution, one of the Council's Assistant Secretaries (A. Dunn Gardner) was seconded in August 1881, to supervise and extend the Society's work in Hackney.[3] In 1882 T. Gage Gardiner was given a similar responsibility at Newington; and at Camber-

[1] Mr Machen at St Saviour's: 21st *Annual Report*, 1889, p. 13. The 7th and 8th *Annual Reports*, 1875 and 1876, contain no reference to this development.

[2] 12th *Annual Report*, 1880 (presented May 4, 1881), pp. 15-16.

[3] 13th *Annual Report*, 1881, p. 17. That the Assistant Secretary was A. D. Gardner is an inference of mine. He, T. G. Gardiner and H. C. Bourne were all Assistant Secretaries that year. T. G. Gardiner was soon appointed to Newington, and Bourne does not seem to have served outside the Central Office.

well 'a superior officer . . . is paid for by the Council'.[1] In that year A. Eveleigh was appointed secretary to the Poplar District Committee.[2] In 1883 the title of District Secretary was first used, being applied to H. V. Toynbee (Hampstead), A. Dunn Gardner (Strand), Eveleigh, T. G. Gardiner, C. Gossett (Camberwell).[3] The Council's justification for these measures is worth quoting:

> Experience shows that the best way of assisting District Committees, most of whose difficulties arise from the lack of men and women of leisure to engage actively in their work, is to place at their disposal for a time, officers well acquainted with the principles and methods of the Society, and able to form a centre for charitable workers and to ensure the thorough execution of all casework. It is better to give this ample assistance to District Committees, as they may require it, for a considerable period, than to pay them visits and to make suggestions when they have not the resources at their command to raise it to the standard adopted by the Council in the Charity Organisation Papers.[4]

By 1884 the Council decided that the plan had been sufficiently tested and it adopted a resolution that

> five suitable paid officers of good education, capacity, and address be appointed after careful selection . . ., each of whom will, with the local Committee to which he may be attached, be responsible for ensuring thoroughness in casework, for enlisting volunteers, and for organising charity.[5]

[1] 13th *Annual Report*, 1881 (presented May 2, 1882), p. 18.
[2] 21st *Annual Report*, 1889, p. 13.
[3] 21st *Annual Report*, 1889, p. 13. This action is not mentioned in the *Annual Reports* for 1884 and subsequent years.
[4] 13th *Annual Report*, 1881, pp. 17-18.
[5] 15th *Annual Report*, 1883, p. 3.

Such officers were to be subject to one year's probation, and were not to be placed in charge of any Committee's work until they had had 'such training as the Administrative Committee shall think fit'. They were officers of the Council, liable to transfer from district to district by the Administrative Committee, but otherwise were under the direction of the District Committee which they were serving for the time being. In 1889 similar qualifications were demanded of paid secretaries of District Committees: they were to be appointed by the Council on the recommendation of the Administrative Committee and on probation, 'as in the case of District Secretaries'. In making such appointments, 'due regard' was to be paid to the wishes of the District Committees.[1]

Out of 40 District Committees in 1889, 10 had District Secretaries and 4 had secretaries. The District Secretaries were H. V. Toynbee (Fulham), H. Davison (St James's, Soho), A. H. Paterson (Clerkenwell), Miss Stewart (Poplar), A. Eveleigh (Bow), W. I. Brooke (St Saviour's, Southwark), C. P. Larner (St Olave's), H. L. Woollcombe (Battersea), Miss Sewell (Camberwell), C. H. Grinling (Woolwich). In 1897 there were 14 District Secretaries (8 men, 6 women) and 8 Secretaries (4 men, 4 women).

The District Secretaries included two veterans in this position, H. V. Toynbee and H. L. Woollcombe. Woollcombe, who joined the staff in 1887, was subsequently Secretary of the C.O.S. from 1919 to 1923. He was a country man from Cornwall, and lived in an old house not far from Par, beloved by all the people of his village, as by the wider circle of members of the C.O.S.[2] H. V. Toynbee was a son of Dr Joseph Toynbee, the pioneer of aural surgery, and brother of Arnold Toynbee, the historian and friend of the working

---

[1] 21st *Annual Report*, 1889, pp. 13-14.
[2] Information from Mrs R. B. Mowat.

man after whom Toynbee Hall was named; and among H. V. Toynbee's children is Arnold Toynbee, the philosophical historian of our own day. He had entered the Society's service in December 1881. In 1898 he and A. H. Paterson (a member of the staff since 1885) were made Organising Secretaries at salaries of £400. Their tasks were to supervise two groups of District Committees, especially in organisation and the training of volunteers.

These appointments reflected the renewed concern, at the end of the century, which the C.O.S. felt for both training for charitable work and popular education about it. Courses of lectures on the history of charity, the poor law and social economy had, indeed, been proposed in 1870. In 1896, the Council outlined a rather Utopian scheme of popular education, misleadingly labelled 'The Training of Volunteers'.

The District Committees should become centres for interesting and training those men of ability and insight who, belonging to the trading and working classes and resident in the neighbourhood, ought by reason of these qualities to have a chief place in the administration of local charity. . . . Thus much of the misunderstanding that prevails in regard to the Society . . . may be removed. . . . In this way by degrees an outer ring of workers may be formed, persons of all classes and professions working in connection with other agencies, but ready to accept the obligation of thoroughness in charity.[1]

In pursuit of this, a Joint Lectures Committee was formed in the autumn of 1896, consisting of representatives of the C.O.S., the Woman's University Settlement in Southwark and the National Union of Women Workers. Lectures were given in London in the autumn and spring of 1896-97, and

[1] 27th *Annual Report*, 1895 (presented March 3, 1896), pp. 43-4.

The Charity Organisation Society

1897-98: some were single lectures, but most of them were series of four. Miss Sewell, of the Women's University Settlement, gave the first series, on 'The scope of charitable work', followed by Miss Miranda Hill on 'The family and character; personal work; co-operation in charity; thoroughness'. Later subjects included the history of the Poor Law, the care of women and children under the Poor Law, the standard of life (Mrs Bosanquet), the Co-operative movement, and a series by different persons on children under the Poor Law, in Reformatories, asylums and special schools. Similar lectures were given in the spring of 1897 and in subsequent seasons in the provinces: in Birmingham, Cheltenham, Gloucester, Malvern, Manchester, Bradford, Norwich, Tunbridge Wells and elsewhere. The committee in 1897 appointed a lecturer, Miss M. McN. Sharpley, at a salary of £150, towards which the Council paid £37, 10s. The committee had its own budget, and financed its work from donations, a grant from the Women's University Settlement, and the proceeds of the lectures. Mrs G. F. Hill was the honorary secretary.[1]

The series of lectures, in London and elsewhere, continued to be given until 1901. One series was devoted to medical relief (London, autumn 1898), another to physical health and recreation; other lectures were on self-help, forethought in charitable work, and similar subjects. Miss Sharpley was probably the busiest lecturer, particularly in the provinces. The venture ended, and the committee was dissolved in September 1901, because the Women's University Settlement felt obliged to withdraw from it as its scope had widened so greatly outside London. Much of the impetus

[1] 28th, 29th and 30th *Annual Report*, 1896-98, pp. 18, 15-16, 11-12 respectively (which give lists of lectures and lecturers); Marjorie J. Smith, *Professional Education for Social Work in Britain: an Historical Account* (Family Welfare Association, 1952), pp. 15-17.

behind the lectures was, however, diverted to a new beginning in the neighbouring area of training.[1]

The work of the C.O.S. in training social workers may be said to date from a paper, 'The Training of Volunteers', read by Mrs Dunn Gardner to the Council on November 26, 1894. District Committees must be convinced, she said, that 'the difficult and troublesome task of Training Volunteer Workers . . . is one of their chief and most important duties. . . .' This was not in order that they might get help in their relief work – indeed, training might often interfere with this. It was because relief work was only a means for the organisation of those by whom the condition of the poor might be improved, and 'each case carefully and efficiently dealt with by a C.O.S. Committee ought to be an object lesson in the best methods of charity'. New workers, accepted with this principle in mind, must first be made interested in the work, and then be given some responsibility. They should be taken through the whole routine of the office, be given letters to answer, casepapers to find and write up, applicants to deal with, loan payments to enter up in the books. They should 'learn as far as possible the duties of a Secretary, so as to be able if required to carry on any of them'. The reading of books (and every District Office had a few books and ought to become a real library) should be part of the training; but the main emphasis in this valuable paper was on training by practical experience, under the supervision of the Secretary and the local Committee.[2]

In the 28th *Annual Report*, for 1896, presented on March 12, 1897, the Council devoted a long section to 'The Education

[1] 33rd *Annual Report*, 1901, pp. 51-4.

[2] Mrs Dunn Gardner, 'The Training of Volunteers', printed in C.O.S. *Occasional Papers*, 1st series, No. 46, and reprinted in Marjorie Smith, *Professional Education for Social Work in Britain*, pp. 45-9 – a most useful and important work on the C.O.S.'s rôle in the beginning of training for social work.

of the Worker'. ' "Training", or the education of the worker, is assuming every year a more prominent place in the work of the Society.' Within the Society, competent volunteers are more and more indispensable; outside, 'as the inutility and harmfulness of ill-regulated relief is acknowledged, a large number of persons desire to learn good methods. Consequently to train volunteers is now the recognised function of many committees.' It distinguished four types of learner: those who come from philanthropic curiosity, those who are *'bona fide* doers', those who are already workers with the Churches or with other charities, and may be won to co-operation with the C.O.S., and, the last small group, those who will continue to work for the Society and may become its leaders. Such training is no part-time job. A Committee will find that 'it will take the whole available time of one or two of its ablest members'. In the reports of District Committees which follow these points are illustrated. The Holborn Committee had given training to ten ladies and gentlemen in the past year. Also, a significant development, several of the Charity Organisation Societies in the provinces had sent members to undergo some weeks' training in one of the London offices.[1]

Soon after this, in May 1897, the Council decided to appoint a Committee on Training. This had been recommended, as the fifth of ten recommendations adopted by the Council from the report of a special committee which had, once again, examined the functions of the District Secretaries. Though inspired by the fear, on the part of some members of the C.O.S., that paid secretaries tended to relieve volunteers of responsibility and relegate them to secondary work, the report recommended the use of paid assistance where necessary to supplement or to make efficient the work of volunteers. The training of volunteers for the position of

[1] 28th *Annual Report*, pp. 15-16, 35.

honorary secretaries should be an essential part of the work of District Secretaries and honorary secretaries. District Committees should send their proposed honorary secretaries for a course of training at other District Offices or at the Central Office. District Secretaries should serve a minimum probationary period of six months and a maximum of twelve months. The fifth resolution asked for the appointment of a committee of specially selected past and present District and Honorary Secretaries 'to study the best practical method of training paid and voluntary workers (such training to include some knowledge of the work of the Central Office)'.[1] This committee was appointed on June 1897, and consisted of W. A. Bailward, A. H. Paterson, R. Sharpe, H. V. Toynbee, A. Wedgwood, H. L. Woollcombe, Miss Bruce and Miss M. Sewell.[2]

The first report of the Committee on Training was adopted by the Council on December 12, 1898. It distinguished two kinds of training: the proseletysing of clergy, district visitors and 'outside workers' of every sort, and the training of executive members of the Society; and it concentrated on the latter. It pointed to the danger caused by 'the Great Development of the Casework of the Society of late years': that the newcomer might never get beyond relief work and so would fail to grasp the principles for which the Society existed. The learner should be impressed with the fact that 'casework is mainly to be used as a means of organisation, and that the "improvement of the condition of the poor" as a whole is a much nobler . . . object'. The suggestions for methods of training which followed were similar to those in Mrs Dunn Gardner's paper of 1894.[3]

[1] 29th *Annual Report*, pp. 18-19.

[2] M. Smith, *Professional Education*, p. 18.

[3] *Ibid.*, pp. 49-51, for extracts from this Report, which appeared in C.O.S. *Occasional Papers*, 2nd series, No. 11; cf. 30th *Annual Report*, 1898, pp. 52-5.

Thus did the Society advance in the theory of training. In the practice of it reliance was still placed on the initiating of the newcomer into the Society's principles and methods under the guidance of the old hands on the District Committees. District secretaries on probation were expected to attend lectures (presumably the Society's series of lectures) and to visit institutions; and prospective secretaries and Honorary Secretaries were encouraged to come to the Central Office for a time to study its work.[1] 'Methods of Training' was the subject of an important paper by Mrs Bosanquet[2] at the C.O.S. conference at the Clothworkers' Hall in London in July 1900.

It is interesting to note that the development of training in the United States occurred at this same time, paralleling or perhaps anticipating the steps taken by the C.O.S. in London. The New York C.O.S. organised a six-week summer training course in 1898, and continued it each summer (for some 30 social workers each session) until in 1903 a winter course was added and in 1904 a year course was begun by the New York School of Philanthropy (forerunner of the New York School of Social Work), which was founded by the C.O.S. The Chicago Institute of Social Science began giving courses in 1903 under Graham Taylor's leadership as part of the extension division of the University of Chicago (in 1908 this became an independent body, the Chicago School of Civics and Philanthropy, which was absorbed by the University in 1920). The School for Social Workers in Baltimore opened its doors in 1904 under the sponsorship of Simmons College and Harvard University.[3]

In London the next step was taken in 1901. When the

[1] 29th *Annual Report*, p. 19.

[2] C.O.S. *Occasional Papers*, 3rd series, No. 3, reprinted in M. Smith, *Professional Education*, pp. 52-5.

[3] J. E. Hagerty, *Training of Social Workers* (New York, 1931), pp. 42-3.

The C.O.S. at the Zenith

Joint Committee on Lectures was dissolved it was replaced by a Special Committee on Social Education, appointed by the Council with much the same membership. The new committee sent out a circular urging the formation of local committees throughout the country, comprising professors of the universities, clergy, Guardians, school teachers, representatives of settlement houses, friendly societies and Charity Organisation societies. The task of these committees was to organise a course of lectures on 'social education' on the twin principles of the importance of the family and the necessity of individual self-support.[1] One result of this circular – which for the first time called for the co-operation of the universities in training for social work – was the founding of the School of Social Science in Liverpool in 1904, under the leadership of Professor E. C. K. Gonner, the University, the Victoria Settlement and the Central Relief and Charity Organisation Society.

Meanwhile, the Committee on Social Education summoned a conference which met in London under Lord Avebury's chairmanship in October 1902. The conference was opened by a stirring speech by Professor Alfred Marshall on 'Economic Teaching at the Universities in Relation to Public Well-being'.[2] It proceeded to discuss the possibilities of combining practical training with university work, but eventually resolved that a Trust ought to be created to provide lectures, teaching and practical work. The Committee was asked to prepare a report suggesting how instruction in the universities in moral science, history and economics could be combined with the work of the Trust, and to sketch a syllabus.[3] The report (a confidential one) was

---

[1] 33rd *Annual Report*, 1901; M. Smith, pp. 23-4.
[2] Reproduced from *C.O. Review*, January 1903, and M. Smith, pp. 55-60.
[3] M. Smith, p. 26.

presented to the Council on June 8, 1903. It discussed courses relevant to social work given in the universities, and particularly at the London School of Economics, but rejected co-operation with the School because of the absence of a 'social and ethical' side to its teaching and because of its conspicuous association 'with one school of thought'. It criticised existing courses as lacking a 'sufficiently practical connection with social problems'. Instead, it proposed a two-year course of training drawn up by E. J. Urwick, combining practical work with lectures and reading on principles, economics and the theory of the structure of society. Poor Law history, theories of the State, and special work in such subjects as sanitation, education, the sick and the imbecile, or in political or economic theory, would form part of the second-year work. An alternative plan, based on the study of labour, industry and commerce, and in the second year concentrating on the family, the child, the adult, women and the aged, was proposed by the Rev. C. F. Rogers. Suggestions for practical training, including three months' daily attendance at a District Office of the C.O.S., were given by Miss Sewell, and supplemented by Mrs Bosanquet. Short courses for charitable workers, men entering the ministry, and Poor Law officers, were also proposed.[1]

As a result of these deliberations, the School of Sociology was opened in October 1903. It was another of the off-shoots of the C.O.S., but was not its own creation: indeed, the subsequent history of this pioneer body for the training of social workers was, from the viewpoint of the C.O.S., something of a tragedy. The school was founded by the Committee on Social Education, but this Committee had, by a resolution of the Council, moved by T. Mackay and passed on July 20, become an independent body, separate from the Society. When the C.O.S. moved its headquarters to Denison

[1] M. Smith, pp. 26-30 60-5, (extracts from the report).

House the School found rooms there also. E. J. Urwick was appointed Lecturer and Tutor, and Mrs G. F. Hill Honorary Secretary of the School. Lectures were given by Urwick, and by various visitors, and practical training provided in the District Offices of the C.O.S.[1] Urwick's introductory lecture emphasised the importance of scientific method and a knowledge of principles and law: particularly the new knowledge of the natural history of society, of social philosophy, social economics and individual and social psychology.[2]

[1] M. Smith, pp. 30, 32; 35th *Annual Report*, 1903, 36th, 1904. Urwick followed the School of Sociology in its move to the London School of Economics in 1912 and subsequently became Professor in the Social Service Department of the University of Toronto. His books include *Luxury and Waste of Life* (1908), *A Philosophy of Social Progress* (1912), *The Social Good* (1927).

[2] M. Smith, pp. 32-3.

CHAPTER VI

Against the Current: the C.O.S. and the Movement of Ideas, 1883-1900

By the middle of the 1880's the climate of opinion in which the C.O.S. had been founded was changing. In the 'seventies there was still a chance that the ideas of the C.O.S. might prevail: that co-operation between Poor Law and private charity, as recommended in the Goschen minute, might develop to the point that the State would not be under pressure to assume new duties in the prevention and relief of poverty; and that the doctrines of individualism, the responsibility of the working man, the newly enfranchised citizen, for the well-being of himself and his family, in bad times as in good, would remain unchallenged.

In this spirit the C.O.S. had supported the movement for the strict administration of the Poor Law which had begun in 1870 and produced in Circular No. 20 of the Local Government Board on 'Out-door Relief' (December 2, 1871), an exhortation to Guardians to apply an efficient workhouse test to all able-bodied applicants for relief.[1] The C.O.S. encouraged members to stand for election as Guardians. It

---

[1] On the history of this movement see S. and B. Webb, *English Poor Law History*, II, i, 435-67, Sir W. Chance's *Better Administration of the Poor Law* (1895), and the 23rd (and last) *Annual Report* of the Poor Law Board, 1871, and the *Annual Reports* of the Local Government Board, especially 1st-3rd, 1872-74; also House of Lords, Select Committee on Poor Law Relief, *Report*, 1888.

commended those Unions which attempted to abolish out-
door relief within their limits. Three such model Unions,
Brixworth, Bradfield and St Georges-in-the-East (in East
London), were much influenced by men who supported the
C.O.S.: Brixworth by Albert Pell, Bradfield by T. Bland
Garland and H. G. Willink, who were successively chairman
of the Board of Guardians, and St Georges by Albert Pell and
A. G. Crowder. Loch and Mackay, in particular, wrote and
spoke frequently on Poor Law matters, not least for the semi-
official Poor Law Conferences – regional gatherings of re-
presentative Guardians – at which strict administration was
generally upheld.[1] Another member of the C.O.S., Sir William
Chance, was Honorary Secretary of the Central Poor Law
Conference, and author of *The Better Administration of the
Poor Law* (1895) in the 'Charity Organisation series', in
which the achievements of the model Unions were described.

In two of these Unions in London the C.O.S. was closely
concerned: St George's-in-the-East and Whitechapel. In St
George's outdoor relief was usually refused, with an impressive reduction in the number of persons receiving such
relief but without any evidence of great hardship. In the
first year, 1875-76, the number on outdoor relief fell from
1799 to 548 without any increase in the number of persons
receiving indoor relief. Many who had applied for relief did
not need it; others had been spurred by the refusal to greater
efforts to find work or to earn more; others had been helped
by charity. Co-operation between the Poor Law and the
C.O.S. was close. So Thomas Mackay of the C.O.S. described
the experiment; critics argued that all that had happened
was that the amount of indiscriminate charity poured into

---

[1] On the Poor Law Conferences see the Webbs, *English Poor Law
History*, II, i, 231-2; the Conferences were reported in a series of
volumes entitled *Poor Law Conferences*, in which the papers and
discussions were reproduced.

the district by various charitable bodies, such as the Salvation Army, had enormously increased.[1] In Whitechapel a similar system was adopted, with co-operation between the Guardians and the C.O.S., under the influence of Canon Barnett and the clerk to the Guardians, W. Vallance; the figures and cost of outdoor relief were greatly reduced (the cost was £7,458 in 1869, £117 in 1888).[2] Much thoughtful charity was dispensed; but 'the flood of indiscriminate charity remained unabated', particularly that of the unofficial 'Jewish Board of Guardians'.[3]

These and several other examples of strict Poor Law administration continued to the time of the Royal Commission on the Poor Laws of 1905-09, but by then they were falling into disfavour or had already been abandoned, and at best they had only involved some 16 Unions in the whole country.[4] Nor was there any enthusiasm to adopt the 'Elberfeld system', although it was twice reported on by the Local Government Board, in 1872 and 1887, on both occasions at the suggestion of William Rathbone. The second report was made by a delegation consisting of C. S. Loch, a C.O.S. official from Liverpool, and J. S. Davy, then an Inspector of the L.G.B.[5]

In the workhouse also strict administration was being tempered by humanity. Workhouse infirmaries were improved, and in London hospitals and asylums had been built by the Metropolitan Asylums Board. Some indulgences were being shown to old people who were forced to spend their closing years in the workhouse.[6] Most significant for future policy, though little noticed at the time, was the removal of

---

[1] T. Mackay, *History of the Poor Law*, III, 558-61; the Webbs, *English Poor Law History*, II, i, 459, 462-4.

[2] C.O.S., *Annual Charities Register and Digest*, 1897, pp. xliii-iv.

[3] Webb, *op. cit.*, 464.   [4] Webb, *op. cit.*, 459-61, 466.

[5] *Ibid.*, 458; L.G.B., *Reports on the Elberfeld Poor Law System* (1888).   [6] Webb, *op. cit.*, 319-26, 349-60.

The C.O.S. and the Movement of Ideas

the stigma of disfranchisement from those who received outdoor medical relief from the Poor Law. This was done by the Medical Relief (Disqualification Removal) Act of 1885; it did not extend to persons who entered the workhouse for medical treatment.[1]

Such changes were part of the new spirit which was becoming manifest in the 'eighties. As the extent of poverty came to be better known, and its causes were seen to lie in impersonal forces quite beyond the range of any man's personal responsibility, the demands for intervention by the State to bring remedies grew until they became irresistible – demands from Conservatives and Liberals almost as much as from the new Socialists of the Labour movement.[2] The C.O.S., for the remainder of Loch's secretaryship, was fighting a rearguard action against 'socialism' and State intervention in the relief of poverty.

We might date the change from the year 1883. In April the Rev. S. A. Barnett, vicar of St Jude's, Whitechapel, where he and his wife had begun their life among the poor in 1873, published an article in the *Nineteenth Century* entitled: 'Practicable Socialism' (a title he subsequently used for a collection of his writings). Barnett was a member of the C.O.S., and had strongly supported the policy of eliminating outdoor relief in Whitechapel. The policy had succeeded, but poverty (if not pauperism) remained: the labourer and his family living on twenty shillings a week.

[1] For the passing of this Act, see Brian Rodgers, 'The Medical Relief (Disqualification Removal) Act, 1885', *Parliamentary Affairs*, IX (1956), 188.

[2] The best accounts of changing opinion are in Gertrude Williams, *The State and the Standard of Living* (1936), Ch. 1, and Helen M. Lynd, *England in the Eighteen-Eighties* (1945). See also Beatrice Webb, *My Apprenticeship*, p. 170 ff. For a most interesting account of similar changes in opinion concerning poverty in the United States at this time see R. H. Bremner, *From the Depths: the Discovery of Poverty in the United States* (New York, 1956).

In the labourer's future there is only the grave and the workhouse. He hardly dares to think at all, for the thought suggests that tomorrow a change in trade or a master's whim may throw him out of work, and leave him unable to pay for rent or for food. The labourers have few thoughts of joy and little hope of rest; it is well for them, if in a day they can obtain ten hours of the dreariest labour, if they can return to a weatherproof room, if they can eat a meal in silence while the children sleep around, and then turn into bed to save light and coal. . . .[1]

It was this life in the East End which (Barnett confessed) had made him a socialist. The State should provide for the poor. It had already accepted much socialistic legislation: the Poor Law, education, the Irish land acts, the Artisans' Dwellings Act among others. It should follow a policy of practicable socialism along these lines: better housing, a national system of education, a proper organisation of medical relief, workhouses used as schools of industry, and pensions for the aged. A graduated system of taxation would provide finance.

Such a picture, and such a solution, became familiar reading in the next few years. Mearns' 'Bitter Cry of Outcast London', published in the *Pall Mall Gazette* in 1883-84, was anything but unique. Every volume of the *Nineteenth Century*, for example, during the 'eighties contained articles on social questions: 'The Great Cities and Social Reform', 'Progress and Wages', 'A Workman's View', Canon Barnett's 'Distress in East London', the young Beatrice Potter's first articles, on dock life in East London (1887), East London labour (chiefly in the tailoring trades), and her 'Pages from a Work-girl's Diary'. Depressions in trade, reaching the bottom of the trough in 1886 and again in 1894, brought

[1] Reprinted in Michael Goodwin, *Nineteenth Century Opinion* (Penguin, 1951).

· 118 ·

unemployment, discontent, strikes, demonstrations; and in 1886 and 1887 the disorders in Trafalgar Square, partly caused by the Social Democratic Federation, gave alarm to the comfortable classes in the heart of the capital. The London dock strike of 1889, with its orderly processions of the strikers, marching through Mayfair with their stinking fish-heads and other emblems of poverty, was another reminder of the poverty existing cheek by jowl with plenty. And Joseph Chamberlain, in his earlier phase as the Radical Jack Cade, had compared the aristocracy to the lilies that 'toil not, neither do they spin', and had asked what ransom property would pay for the security it enjoyed.

Socialism was, of course, another challenge to accepted ideas, and one which was to be bitterly opposed by the C.O.S. in later years. The Social Democratic Federation, founded in 1881, and the Fabian Society (1884), by demanding a new and more equal distribution of property, aimed to sweep away a social order in which poverty and charity could exist. They refused to regard poverty as the natural lot of a great part of the nation. The early *Fabian Tracts*, and *Fabian Essays* (1889), did not, however, devote much attention to the relief of poverty nor propose any suggestion of a welfare State: the Poor Law should be reorganised under the municipal and local authorities, the stigma attaching to relief should be removed, but for the able-bodied help should be given only on condition that work was done or training accepted.[1] More disturbing at the time was Henry George's *Progress and Poverty*, and his great lecture tours in Great Britain in 1882, 1884 and 1888. Nor were the poor without friends in highly respectable circles. Two Anglican societies, the Guild of St Matthew and the Christian Social Union, were proclaiming the social duty of the Church of England.

[1] *Fabian Essays* (1920 edition), p. 55 (Sidney Webb quoting and endorsing the Radical programme from the *Star*, August 8, 1888).

The Charity Organisation Society

Among the Roman Catholics – who included the thousands of Irish immigrants who gravitated to low-paid jobs of unskilled labour in the docks and elsewhere – Cardinal Manning was a champion of the rights of labour.

Nor must we forget the influence on poverty, charity and relief of the advance of democracy. It was not so much the Reform Act of 1884 as the Local Government Act of 1894 which presaged a new order. By extending the local government franchise and abolishing the property qualification for Poor Law Guardians it opened the way for working men to be elected to the Boards of Guardians. The new type of Guardian might, of course, be more strict towards his fellow-men than the older Guardians, of a different social class, had sometimes been, but he might also be more sympathetic and unwisely generous: of which the C.O.S. expressed some fear.

The belief that all was not well was soon reinforced by Charles Booth's pioneering social investigation of the lives of the poor in East London. Here was an enterprise in harmony with the beliefs of the C.O.S.: a study based on the careful investigation and classifying of the facts and on the examination of the circumstances of innumerable families in their own homes. Yet its conclusions led Booth, and a great many other people, toward policies of State intervention which the C.O.S. did its utmost to resist. The first part of what was eventually the seventeen volumes of the *Life and Labour of the People of London* appeared as *Labour and Life of the People* in 1889, and showed, on the basis of house-to-house inquiries and the testimony of School Board visitors, C.O.S. workers and others, that 30 per cent. of the population was living in poverty. The causes were various: crime, immorality, drink, laziness, mental weakness, early marriages, extravagance; but also low wages, the death of the bread-winner or the wife, sickness and accidents, and old age. The public alarm was heightened by the evidence of the conditions of work and wages in the sweated industries of London, as revealed by the report of the Select Committee of the House of Lords on the Sweating System in 1890. It was no far cry to Bernard Shaw's declaration in the preface to *Major Barbara* in 1906 that 'the greatest of evils and the worst of crimes is poverty, and our first duty . . . is not to be poor'.[1]

The prevalence of low wages was given prominence at an unusual conference held at Prince's Hall, Piccadilly, in London, on January 28-30, 1885, the Industrial Remuneration Conference. This was held, under Sir Charles Dilke's chairmanship, under the terms of a bequest of £1,000 for inquiring whether the existing distribution of the products of industry was satisfactory, and how it could be improved. Sir Thomas Brassey argued that there had been real progress, raising the standard of life of the working class while diminishing the profits of capital. A paper by Miss Edith Simcox argued the opposite, that the chief benefits of industrial progress had been reaped by the largest capitalists, employers, traders, and the most skilled workmen: both the prizes for success and the penalties of failure had been increased. Miss Simcox estimated that there were five million people whose maximum wages barely sufficed for the necessaries and decencies of life; any mischance plunged them into penury. Another speaker declared that agricultural labourers in Wiltshire were worse off on 10s. a week then than they had been on 7s. a week fifty years before; food for a family in the workhouse would cost 15s.[2]

In this setting, demands for State intervention for the prevention and relief of poverty inevitably grew. The largest and most exhaustive inquiry into social conditions during

[1] G. B. Shaw, *John Bull's Other Island and Major Barbara* (1908), p. 154.
[2] *Charity Organisation Review*, February 1885.

The Charity Organisation Society

these years was made by the Royal Commission on Labour (1892-94), whose 49 volumes included reports on labour conditions in several foreign countries, minutes of evidence of a most detailed sort on hours and wages in the main industries, digests of the evidence prepared by the indefatigable secretary, Geoffrey Drage, and elaborate indices of persons and subjects which provided additional précis of the evidence. The Commission was an influential one, presided over by the Duke of Devonshire and including several politicians and trade unionists, and Alfred Marshall the economist. Its mandate was to inquire into the questions of labour relations, combinations of employers and employed and conditions of labour which had been raised by the trade disputes at the beginning of the'nineties. The majority report was principally a summary of the facts of these subjects, and its recommendations were largely negative: against statutory boards of conciliation and arbitration and a maximum working day established by law.

The minority report, signed by four trade unionists, Tom Mann, J. Mawdsley, William Abraham and Michael Austin, sounded a different, warning note. Five million persons earned insufficient money for adequate subsistence; two million people were driven upon the Poor Law each year; London, the world's wealthiest city, had 32 per cent. of its people living below Booth's poverty line; one person in three over 70 was in receipt of relief. Moreover, two-thirds of the annual product of the community was absorbed by a quarter of its members; and the annual tribute of rent, royalties and dividends levied on the industry of the nation was nearly £5 millions. The report demanded action against the sweated industries, better factory inspection, an eight-hour day prescribed by law as the maximum for every manual worker. It ascribed the unsatisfactory relations of employers and employed to the present industrial anarchy.

The C.O.S. and the Movement of Ideas

'The only complete solution of the problem is, in our opinion, to be found in the progress of the industrial evolution, which will assign to the "captains of industry", as well as to the manual workers, their proper position as servants of the community.'[1]

Regulation and intervention were also being increasingly justified by the economists. John Stuart Mill's partial conversion to socialism under Harriet Taylor's influence is well known: 'We yet looked forward to a time when society will no longer be divided into the idle and the industrious; when the rule that they who do not work shall not eat, will be applied not to paupers only, but impartially to all; when the division of the produce of labour, instead of depending, as in so great a measure it now does, on the accident of birth, will be made by consent on an acknowledged principle of justice. . . . '[2] Stanley Jevons, in the preface to *The State in Relation to Labour* (1882), seemed to argue that the choice between *laissez-faire* and intervention was purely subjective: 'the all-important point is to explain if possible why, in general, we uphold the rule of *laissez-faire*, and yet in large classes of cases invoke the interference of local or central authorities . . . the outcome of the inquiry is that we can lay down no hard-and-fast rules, but must treat every case in detail upon its merits'.[3]

Alfred Marshall's views, the more weighty as coming from the professor of political economy at Cambridge, were decidedly subversive of the old orthodoxies. The modern view of the distribution of wealth, he argued in the first volume of his *Principles of Economics* (1890), involved a

[1] R.C. on Labour, *Fifth and Final Report*, C. 7421, 1894 (P.P., 1894, v. 35), p. 146.

[2] J. S. Mill, *Autobiography* (World's Classics edition, p. 196), quoted in W. H. B. Court, *Concise Economic History of Britain from 1750 to Recent Times* (1954), p. 252.

[3] Quoted in Court, p. 253.

fundamental change from the beginning of the century. A man's character and efficiency were no longer thought to be a fixed quantity, but were the product of his circumstances. 'Broadly speaking,' he declared, 'the destruction of the poor is their poverty', and poverty was not necessary. What was needed were restraints which would defend the weak in matters where they could not use the forces of competition in their defence.[1] In his memorandum and evidence before the Royal Commission on the Aged Poor (1893-95), Marshall went further in justifying State action to mitigate poverty. He scorned the idea that the methods of the Poor Law and charity left little suffering beyond what was needed to educate people to braver and stronger lives: 'such patience appears excessive to persons who, like myself, think that there are still many hardships which cost more pain than they are worth for the purposes of education'.[2] He attacked the theory that public aid given to some people lowers the wages of the rest: rather, by raising the standard of living it increases consumption and so employment and wages.[3] He added:

> As regards this a change has come, which separates the economics of this generation from the economics of the past; but it seems to me not to have penetrated the Poor Law literature yet. . . . While the problem of 1834 was the problem of pauperism, the problem of 1893 is the problem of poverty; that a man ought not to be allowed to live in a bad home, that extreme poverty ought to be regarded, not indeed as a crime, but as a thing so detrimental to the State that it should not be endured.[4]

[1] G. Williams, *State and the Standard of Living*, p. 18.
[2] *Official Papers by Alfred Marshall*, p. 203.
[3] R.C. on the Aged Poor, *Minutes of Evidence*, C. 7684 – I and II, 1895, Q. 10272.
[4] *Ibid.*, Q. 10272, 10358.

The C.O.S. and the Movement of Ideas

This was, of course, to oppose the individualist ideas which, in their purest form, were expressed by Herbert Spencer. In *Man versus the State* (1884) Spencer inveighed against 'the coming slavery', the assumption 'that there should be no suffering, and that society is to blame for that which exists'. The command ' "if any would not work neither should he eat" is simply a Christian enunciation of that universal law of Nature under which life has reached its present height. . . . '[1] In the revised edition (1892) of *Social Statics*, first published in 1865, he repeated the argument that man could be self-sufficing provided he was adaptable and efficient, as he would become under necessity. 'Would you draw out and increase some feeble sentiment? Then you must set it to do, as well as it can, the work required of it. It must be kept ever active, ever strained, ever inconvenienced by its incompetence. Under this treatment it will, in the slow course of generations, attain to efficiency.'[2]

The C.O.S.'s most redoubtable champion of individualism was Mrs Bosanquet. Her *Strength of the People* is a long sermon on the importance of character in making one family rich and another poor. The best way to help the poor is to make them efficient: the greater the number of skilled workmen, earning good wages, the greater the increase of consumption which, in turn, will demand more skilled labour.

The remedy against the extension of pauperism does not lie in the liberalities of the rich. It lies in the hearts and habits of the poor. Plant in their bosoms a principle of independence. Give a higher tone of delicacy to their character. Teach them to recoil from pauperism as a degradation.

For, she adds, 'the root of the matter lies in the fact that

[1] H. Spencer, *Man versus the State* (ed. of 1908, New York), p. 303.
[2] H. Spencer, *Social Statics*, Abridged and Revised (ed. of 1918, New York), pp. 125-6.

without independence there can be no real ability to serve others'. And that spirit of independence will become enervated by state assistance: help, to be beneficial, must be a mutual giving and receiving.[1] She even entered into controversy with Alfred Marshall, who had asked in *Political Economy* 'whether it is necessary that there should be any so-called lower classes at all – that is, whether there need be large numbers of people doomed from their birth to hard work in order to provide for others the requisites of a refined and cultured life, while they themselves are prevented by their poverty and toil from having any share or part in that life'. Her answer was that the lowest paid workers were employed on goods for the poor, such as cheap clothes, not on luxury articles for the rich.[2]

In another passage Mrs Bosanquet ascribes overcrowding to the lack of a sense of responsibility on the part of those enduring it.

> But what if the social conditions will not permit them to meet the responsibility? It is a vain and idle hypothesis. The social conditions *will* permit them; for their very effort to do so will make them steady and efficient workers, whose services will be valued by the community, and will be supplemented by the help of the young people who will grow up in such a family as theirs will be. On the other hand, nothing is so easy as to undermine this sense of responsibility, and draw the very sap out of a man's life.[3]

The growing differences between the C.O.S. and other persons concerned with poverty and its relief – the increasing

[1] Helen Bosanquet, *Strength of the People* (2nd ed., 1903), pp. 120-3.
[2] *Ibid.*, pp. 70-1 (see also correspondence between herself and Marshall in the introduction).
[3] *Ibid.*, pp. 208-9, quoted in Gertrude Williams, *State and the Standard of Living*, pp. 11-12.

unpopularity in which the C.O.S. worked – were brought out in a clash between Canon Barnett and C. S. Loch at a meeting of the Council of the C.O.S. on July 15, 1895, at which Barnett read a paper entitled 'A friendly criticism of the C.O.S.'. The Barnetts had originally been strong supporters of C.O.S. principles. 'Relief, if it is to be helpful, must strengthen and not weaken character', he wrote in 1884. He was much opposed to the Mansion House Fund of 1885-86 and 'the irresponsible and indiscriminate provision of meals, lodging and other doles', to schemes which did not separate the honest unemployed from the 'demoralised residuum'. In the bad winter of 1880-81 he had supported the 'Whitechapel policy' of providing generous weekly payments, through the C.O.S., to distressed families provided the father went into the workhouse. As founder and first warden of Toynbee Hall in 1884 he was really applying C.O.S. ideas to social work, since he was providing a means by which more fortunate people could live among the poor, instead of merely conducting 'missions' to them, and could give them their friendship and their help in classes and clubs.[1]

Barnett had come to believe that action by the state was indispensable if the problems of unemployment and the aged poor were to be dealt with effectively. His quarrel with the C.O.S. was, therefore, that it had not moved with him, and with the times. In 1888, when some C.O.S. people rejected a proposal of his for a training farm for unemployed men, he wrote 'they were just impossible – refusing to do anything except clothe themselves in the dirty rags of their own righteousness. *They* were based on the true principles. . . .' In 1894 he complained in an article, 'Christianity and the Charity Organisation Society' that the Society

[1] Henrietta O. Barnett, *Canon Barnett: His Life, Work and Friends* (1919), II, 229-35, 239; S. A. Barnett, 'The Universities and the Poor', *Nineteenth Century*, February 1884.

did not always enquire into the causes of a family's poverty in Christ's spirit of tenderness: human beings were too often regarded as 'cases'.[1]

Speaking before the Council in 1895, Barnett charged that, in spite of the devoted work of the District Committees, the C.O.S. was out of sympathy with the forces shaping the times, and was no longer leading or helping to form opinion. Charity, he charged, was as disorganised, poverty as prevalent, as when the Society was founded. Thousands were now receiving public aid, in the Board Schools and in Poor Law infirmaries, without being demoralised. Why should a State pension be more degrading than one provided by a neighbour (or by the Society)? Is thrift always so virtuous? Saving 'may be a crime'. 'The frugal home with possibly the hard unloving mother, and the scheming successful father, is . . . placed above . . . the home ruled by generous and hospitable instincts.' When State pensions are suggested, the Council 'at once hurls this stone: "Outdoor relief is bad, and State pensions are an extreme and very mischievous form of out-relief"'.[2] When municipal work for the unemployed is proposed the Council withdraws from the Committee 'to save its garments from pollution'; it 'could not be a party to any scheme for increasing the habitual dependence of the poor'.[3] The trouble was that C.O.S. principles had degenerated into dogma, and members of the Council had become idolators, worshipping such idols as saving and independence from State relief. The Council 'has become the expounder of a certain way of charity and is not the voice of living growing charity of the time. It condemns more than it organises, it sometimes despises where it ought to woo. . . . It

[1] H. O. Barnett, *Canon Barnett*, II, 265-6.

[2] *Ibid.*, 266-7; S. A. Barnett, 'A friendly criticism of the C.O.S.', *Charity Organisation Review*, August, 1895, pp. 338-42.

[3] *C.O. Review*, August 1895, p. 340, citing *Annual Reports* of C.O.S. for 1891 and 1892.

has a sort of panic at the suggestion of socialism.' Could it not, instead, catch and guide 'the goodwill and enthusiasm now so prevalent'?[1]

A fairly good-natured discussion followed until Loch rose in rebuttal, delivering a speech considerably longer than Barnett's. He was evidently very angry, and treated Barnett's speech as 'an attack upon himself personally'. Barnett was 'an actual, and in part also, a declared opponent to the whole policy of the Society'. 'With Mr Barnett,' he continued, 'progress is a series of reactions. He must be in harmony with the current philanthropic opinion of the moment or perhaps just a few seconds ahead of it. . . . He . . . sails close to the philanthropic winds . . . having changed once or more than once [he] may yet change once again.' Loch went on to defend the record and achievements of the C.O.S., to enlarge on the pensions it provided and to attack State pensions. He concluded on the same personal note. Barnett 'has not proved his case, and (I do not, perhaps, use too strong a word) the bitterness of his attack indicates how far he has drifted away from those who were once his fellow-workers'.[2]

Yet it was not only idealists like Barnett who were becoming critical of the C.O.S. Alfred Marshall, in his evidence before the Royal Commission on the Aged Poor, said that it was 'necessarily oligarchic'. Its members 'have taken upon themselves one of the most important functions that the State can have; and yet they belong to the old world, in this way, that their basis consists exclusively of those people who used to be the governing classes but who are not the governing classes now'.[3] A different criticism

[1] *Ibid.*, pp. 340, 342-3.
[2] *Ibid.*, pp. 364, 371; H. O. Barnett, *Canon Barnett*, II, 267, quoting from the *Westminster Gazette*, September 20, 1895, which said: 'Mr Loch led off with a somewhat vehement personal assault upon Canon Barnett himself'.
[3] R.C. on Aged Poor, *Min. of Ev.*, Q. 10210.

The Charity Organisation Society

may be given in the words of Mr Goult, a Poplar Guardian, in rebutting at a C.O.S. meeting charges of lax administration in a labour yard: 'the C.O.S. stunk in the nostrils of the working men; that it spent £25 in office expenses for every £5 that went to the poor'.[1]

With this we may compare a later criticism of the C.O.S. Beatrice Webb, before her marriage, came across the C.O.S. in her work in East London in the 'eighties as a social investigator and, briefly, as a rent-collector in buildings near St Katherine's Dock which were managed on Octavia Hill's lines.[2] Loch, who met her in 1886, wrote:

> I met Miss Beatrice Potter at the South Inquiry Committee today. I have heard of her before, perhaps met her. I suppose she would do things well. Dark haired, dark-eyed, pale complexion and striking-looking. . . .[3]

Writing her reminiscences many years later, Beatrice Webb praised the C.O.S. as 'an honest though short-circuited attempt to apply the scientific method of observation and experiment, reasoning and verification, to the task of delivering the poor from their miseries by the personal service and pecuniary assistance tendered by their leisured and wealthy fellow-citizens'.[4] She recognised the merits of its principles of personal service, personal responsibility, and casework, but criticised its 'obsession' that the 'mass-misery of great cities arose mainly, if not entirely, from spasmodic, indiscriminate and unconditional doles, whether in the form of alms or in that of Poor Law relief'. It led to the concentration of help upon the 'deserving', in spite of the fact that it was difficult, if not impossible, to define the deserving, and that classification by merit had no relation to classification

[1] *C.O. Review*, January, 1896, p. 40.
[2] B. Webb, *My Apprenticeship*, p. 252 ff.
[3] C. S. Loch to his wife, May 7, 1886.
[4] B. Webb, *My Apprenticeship*, p. 189.

by need. Moreover, personal friendship with the poor was difficult when the visitor was an 'intruder in the poor man's hovel, mixing rigorous questioning . . . with expressions of friendly sympathy . . .'. The 'well-to-do men and women of goodwill . . . found themselves transformed into a body of amateur detectives'; they calmly assumed a 'social and mental superiority over the poor', and lacked ' "the consciousness of collective sin" '. Thus the C.O.S. became 'the most exclusive of sects, making a merit of disapproving and denouncing much of the practice of other charitable agencies, while failing to obtain the means to cope with the 'vast ocean of poverty' on its own terms. As public opinion shifted from concern with the relief of poverty to the work of preventing destitution by the use of the powers of the State, the C.O.S. was left behind; its refusal to co-operate with the development of alternative measures of its own led to its decline and failure.[1]

*   *   *   *   *

In the 1890's there were two kinds of State intervention which were being more insistently demanded and which Loch and the C.O.S., despite the changing climate of opinion, as vigorously resisted. They were measures for the relief of unemployment, and old age pensions, both outside the Poor Law.

Unemployment, more especially in London, was of two kinds: the chronic under-employment of men and women on the fringe of the labour force – dockers, unskilled labourers, and particularly those in the building trades where seasonal lay-offs were common, and women in the sweated industries: and the more general unemployment which appeared in times of depression. That London, more than most of the large

---

[1] *Ibid.*, pp. 194-99; S. and B. Webb, *English Poor Law History*, II, i, 456, 468. Cf. G. D. H. Cole in A. F. C. Bourdillon, *Voluntary Social Services*, pp. 19-20.

British cities, was the scene of both these types of unemployment had a decisive influence on the thought of the C.O.S. on unemployment. It meant that the C.O.S. opposed relief works, or other schemes for the relief of the able-bodied outside the Poor Law, in normal times, on the ground that work was available, and that the needy should be encouraged to look for it, and would only be demoralised if easy help, without the deterrent quality of the Poor Law, were offered them. In abnormal times of more general unemployment the C.O.S. admitted the need of special arrangements;[1] but the very term it used, 'exceptional distress', hampered it in coming to grips with the general problem of unemployment, not all of which was either exceptional or of the chronic type existing on the fringe of the labour market.

The C.O.S.'s own prescription for dealing with exceptional distress was for the Society and other charitable bodies to work with the Poor Law in providing relief while the need lasted; as in Whitechapel and elsewhere in London in the severe winter of 1880-81, and again in 1894-95. In the winter of 1885-86, however, came the catastrophe of the Mansion House Relief Fund: over £70,000 raised from the public, and doled out without system by emergency committees, so that the deserving and the self-effacing received little or nothing while those without need, and the 'ne'er-do-wells from all parts of the country [who] flocked to London'[2] to obtain 'their share', scrambled for the largesse. None was stronger in his condemnation of the harm done by this fund than Canon Barnett.[3]

---

[1] For the best statement of this, see Board of Trade, Labour Department, *Report on Agencies and Methods for dealing with the Unemployed*, C. 7182, 1893, pp. 146-7.

[2] Mrs Barnett's words: H. O. Barnett, *Canon Barnett*, II, 234.

[3] *Ibid.*, pp. 235-6; cf. C.O.S., 18th *Annual Report*, 1886, pp. 13-16.

The C.O.S. and the Movement of Ideas

The emergency caused the C.O.S. in 1886 to set up a special committee 'on the best means of dealing with exceptional distress'. Its report, in the Society's usual government blue-book form, included lengthy minutes of evidence given by members of the District Committees and others describing the working of the Mansion House Fund and the other agencies of relief. Albert Pell was chairman, Rev. Brooke Lambert, J. H. Allen, J. R. Holland, the Hon. C. W. Fremantle, E. Peters, F. J. S. Edgcombe, Dr G. B. Longstaff, the Rev. M. S. A. Walrond, A. G. Crowder, George Shipton (of the London Trades Council) and others were members. The report opposed the establishment of a central relief fund but favoured public and charitable 'works' if prepared for in advance, entrusted to local 'conjoint' committees (including voluntary societies and the local authorities), and managed according to definite rules and paying contract rates of wages.[1]

The most important product of the report was the 'suggestions and suggested rules for dealing with exceptional distress by local committees'. This classified men in need as (i) thrifty and careful, (ii) men of differing grades of responsibility, non-provident, but with a decent home, (iii) the idle, loafing class, and those brought low by drink or vice. Those in class (i) should be assisted by charity, or helped to emigrate, or recommended for employment on the public works; at any rate, should be kept out of the workhouse. Men in class (ii) might be recommended to the public works, or, following the Whitechapel 'modified workhouse test', might be given charitable aid for their families on condition that they themselves entered the workhouse. Those in class (iii) should be left to the Poor Law, unless there were strong reasons for not breaking up the family, in which case

[1] C.O.S., *On the Best Means of Dealing with Exceptional Distress: the Report of a Special Committee*, November 1886.

the modified-workhouse test might be applied to them also.[1]

While the C.O.S. was thus diffidently compromising with the idea of relief works started in times of exceptional distress (which Loch opposed in evidence before public inquiries in the 'nineties), the government in 1886 openly recommended the use of local relief works to give help to the unemployed. During his brief term at the Local Government Board in Gladstone's third government, Joseph Chamberlain issued a circular on March 15, 1886, concerning municipal relief works. Anticipating that 'large numbers of persons usually in regular employment will be reduced to the greatest straits . . . if the depression in trade continues', it urged local authorities to provide relief work which would not involve the 'stigma of pauperism'. Works such as street-cleaning, laying out of streets and open places, paving, sewerage schemes, should be undertaken, using men engaged on the recommendation of the Guardians. Such men would not be receiving relief from the Guardians, and would thus not be disfranchised. It was undesirable that the working classes should be familiarised with Poor Law relief; rather, 'the spirit of independence which leads so many of the working classes to make such great personal sacrifices rather than incur the stigma of pauperism' should be encouraged, and the Poor Law left to provide for ordinary pauperism.[2]

Here was a major innovation. The problem of unemploy-

[1] *Ibid.*, also Board of Trade, Labour Department, *Report on Agencies for Dealing with the Unemployed*, 1893, pp. 151-3; C.O.S., 19th *Annual Report*, 1887, App. IV (also Charity Organisation Paper No. 5). See also *Suggestions and Suggested Rules for dealing with Exceptional Distress by Local Committees.* December 1889 (Charity Organisation Paper, No. 11).

[2] Board of Trade, *Report on Agencies*, 1893, p. 185. On this and other aspects of early policy toward the unemployed, see S. and B. Webb, *English Poor Law History*, II, ii, 631-49; W. H. Beveridge, *Unemployment, A Problem of Industry* (1909), pp. 150-9.

ment was recognised, and the Poor Law set aside in dealing with it. The man who had hitherto avoided Poor Law assistance was to be kept free of it, be given public help but not to the impairment of his citizenship. The policy was akin to that of the C.O.S. in keeping the respectable working man off the Poor Law, but did so by the use of public rather than charitable funds. It also demanded a new discrimination of the relieving officers or the Guardians in dealing with applicants for relief – something of the casework approach. In fact the policy, reiterated in several circulars, was little followed: by only 73 authorities out of 673 which were asked for reports.

Some efforts to provide relief work in winter by private agencies were made in the next few years. A Mansion House Conference considered the question in the spring and summer of 1888, and examined the experience of the Public Gardens Association in offering work for the unemployed. It found that of 456 men offered work, 62 failed to appear, 134 were dismissed for misconduct, absences or incapacity, 164 proved unhelpable, leaving only 96, or 22 per cent., who were helped in a positive way, either by emigration (in the case of 26), or being tided over until they obtained better employment.[1] In the winter of 1892-93 a Mansion House Conference took place as an outgrowth of the Toynbee Commission, a body including residents of Toynbee Hall and representatives of the trade unions and the C.O.S., which investigated conditions in East London. The Conference obtained some waste land at Abbey Mills and offered work to the unemployed in laying it out for allotments. 372 men applied for help, 96 were rejected, 224 employed, of whom 124 were reported as 'good' workers, 59 as 'fair'. Cases were inquired into and help given on C.O.S. principles, but the C.O.S. withdrew from the management committee, in which

[1] C.O.S., 20th *Annual Report*, 1888, pp. 25-7.

Loch and Sir Charles Fremantle, chairman of the Council, served, when it refused to employ men only on piece-work – the incident referred to by Canon Barnett in his address to the C.O.S. in 1895.[1]

Loch and the C.O.S. also found themselves in disagreement with 'General' William Booth's scheme for helping the unemployed as expounded in his *In Darkest England and the Way Out*, published in 1890. The scheme – though it had many other ramifications – proposed to give immediate relief in 'city colonies', whence men would be sent to 'farm colonies' for training, and eventually to 'overseas colonies' and permanent settlement. Loch, though approving many of the principles of the scheme, and particularly its emphasis on character, criticised its statistics, the expense and limited value of the farm colonies, and its duplication with work already being done by other bodies. The first two parts of this scheme were partially realised in the Salvation Army's workshops (called 'Elevators') and its farm colony at Hadleigh.[2]

By the latter part of the 'nineties the government was showing even more concern for the unemployed, though still holding back from any systematic intervention on their behalf. The Board of Trade Labour Department issued a useful *Report on Agencies and Methods for dealing with the Unemployed* in 1893.[3] It described the work of 'Labour

[1] Board of Trade, *Report on Agencies for dealing with the Unemployed*, pp. 238-43; C.O.S., 25th *Annual Report*, 1893, pp. 10-11, 38-41; H. O. Barnett, *Canon Barnett*, II, 238-40.

[2] C. S. Loch, *An Examination of 'General' Booth's Social Scheme* (1890); C. S. Loch, Bernard Bosanquet, Canon Philip Dwyers, *Criticisms on 'General' Booth's Social Scheme* (1891). There are other pamphlets opposing the scheme by T. H. Huxley and W. Hazlitt Roberts, and in favour of it by H. Greenwood. See also John Manson, *The Salvation Army and its Work* (1906), for criticism of the Salvation Army's finances and work.

[3] C. 7182, 1893.

The C.O.S. and the Movement of Ideas

Bureaux', labour colonies in Germany, Belgium, Holland and elsewhere and the experience of municipal relief works; it recounted the efforts of trade unions, friendly societies, the Salvation Army, the Girls' Friendly Society, the Metropolitan Association for Befriending Young Servants ('Mabys') and similar voluntary and commercial agencies, in finding work for those in need of it; and it gave prominence to the ideas and methods of the C.O.S. The Royal Commission on Labour was concerned incidentally with unemployment, but more with irregular employment. It heard evidence from Loch on Dutch labour colonies and relief works; he deprecated the provision of artificial employment by public bodies, and suggested that unemployment would be a less serious matter if families would exercise foresight to have money in hand to tide them over bad times.[1] In 1896 the Select Committee of the House of Commons on Distress from Want of Employment made its report. It recommended against helping the unemployed by grants from the Treasury. However, it recognised the special character of the problem by proposing that an unemployed man should not be disfranchised for receiving relief provided it was for less than one month in a year. Once again, Loch was a witness. He urged the importance of co-operation between the Poor Law and private charity, stressed the danger of pauperism and held up St George's-in-the-East and Shoreditch (where little or no outdoor relief was given) as examples to the other Metropolitan unions whose expenditures on relief had risen sharply in 1895.[2]

The movement for old age pensions brought the C.O.S. into yet another defensive action against a new force invading

[1] R.C. on Labour, *Min. of Evidence before the Royal Commission* (sitting as a whole), C. 7063-II, 1893. Q. 58-59; cf. *Indexes*, v. 4.

[2] Report of Select Committee on *Distress from Want of Employment*, 1896 (P.P., 1896, v. 9).

the preserves of individualism and private charity. It began in 1878 with the proposal of the Rev. W. L. Blackley, incumbent of North Waltham, Hampshire (later Honorary Canon of Winchester), for National Insurance. His was a proposal for compulsory insurance: payments by every young man and woman between the ages of 18 and 21 would produce about £10 per head which would provide a pension of 4s a week at 70, and a sickness allowance of 8s. a week before 70. His initial article in the *Nineteenth Century* (November 1878) was followed by a campaign of speaking and writing sustained for many years, partly under the auspices of the National Providence League.[1] A different and much less well-known proposal was that of R. P. Hookham of Islip, Oxfordshire; in *Outlines of a Scheme for dealing with Pauperism* (1897) he proposed non-contributory old age pensions payable to all persons, regardless of means or savings, as a right rather than a favour.[2]

By the 'nineties there were many schemes in the field, the most prominent being those advocated by Charles Booth and Joseph Chamberlain. Booth proposed to cut through all the arguments against old age pensions – the discouragement of thrift, the difficulty of discriminating between the deserving and needy and the undeserving, the stigma of pauperism and the damage to independence in receiving a pension – by granting to everyone a non-contributory pension of 5s. a week at 65 or 70. He scouted the argument that this was socialism: so was much of the social legislation of the last hundred years. He admitted that universal pensions at 70 would cost £20 millions a year: 'I know of no way or ways in which an expenditure of up to twenty millions a year could be so well

---

[1] Sir Arnold Wilson and G. S. Mackay, *Old Age Pensions: an historical and critical study* (Oxford, 1941), pp. 9, 14-16.

[2] *Ibid.*, pp. 9-10; cf. Charles Booth, *Old Age Pensions* (1899), pp. 71-5.

applied to the welfare of the whole people.'[1] He was no socialist himself: his motive was to strengthen individualism by removing a burden – provision for old age by the poor – which it could not sustain.[2] Chamberlain offered three types of voluntary, contributory pension schemes: one would pay 5s. a week at 65, the second would, for higher contributions, add benefits for widows and children; the third would double, by a contribution from the State, any pension payable through savings in a friendly society. His motives were similar to Booth's. 'The first is that there is a very large number of people who have led ordinary respectable lives but who in old age are forced to go upon the Poor Rates, and I think that that is reasonably felt to be a scandal upon our civilisation.' The second was that once the aged poor had been removed from its rolls, the Poor Law could be more stringently administered.[3]

In addition, Bismarck's 'state socialism' seemed to furnish an example for Great Britain and was avowedly conservative in intention. In return for compulsory payments over 30 years a very small pension (in many cases below 5s. a week) might be claimed at 70. W. H. Dawson's *Bismarck and State Socialism*, which expounded this and other Bismarckian schemes, went into a second edition in its first year of publication, 1891. In New Zealand – distant but British – a non-contributory old age pension of 7s. per week at 65 for those in need was instituted in 1898 and provided another precedent.

[1] C. Booth, *Old Age Pensions*, p. 70. This small book gives Booth's principal arguments; cf. his *Pauperism, A Picture;* and *The Endowment of Old Age, an Argument* (1892), and *The Aged Poor in England and Wales* (1894).

[2] B. Webb, *My Apprenticeship*, p. 222.

[3] Royal Commission on the Aged Poor, *Evidence*, v. 3, C. 7684—II (P.P., 1895, v. 15), Q. 12170; quoted in A. Wilson, *Old Age Pensions*, p. 26.

The Charity Organisation Society

In 1893 the Liberal government appointed the Royal Commission on the Aged Poor to consider whether any alterations were desirable in the Poor Law as it affected aged destitute persons, 'or whether assistance could otherwise be afforded in those cases'. The chairman was Lord Aberdare; the Prince of Wales was a member and took an active part in its examination of witnesses. Loch and Albert Pell, of the C.O.S., were members; also Charles Booth, Chamberlain, C. T. Ritchie, Joseph Arch, Henry Broadhurst. The majority report (which Loch and Pell signed) devoted much attention to the Poor Law's provision for the aged. It put the number of persons over 65 who were supported by the Poor Law at 268,397 (one-day count, January 1, 1892). This was 19·8 per cent. of the total population of England and Wales over 65; the proportion of the total population of all ages which was on relief was only 2·4 per cent. Of the aged poor on relief only 63,352 were on indoor relief. In London 35 per cent. of the population over 65 were supported by the Poor Law, and of these 23 per cent. were on indoor relief. The proportion of the working-class population over 65 on relief was, as the Report[1] observed, obviously much higher.

The majority's recommendations were cautious. The members favoured giving outdoor relief to the aged poor, and insisted that it should be adequate; and they urged that old people who came into the workhouse should be given greater freedom regarding hours of rising and retiring, visitors, absences to pay visits, type of clothes, food and personal comforts; they insisted that (as the law permitted) aged married couples should not be separated except at their own request. They stipulated that the test of destitution should be retained, and for those given outdoor relief should be coupled with 'evidence of respectability and a reasonable

[1] R.C. on Aged Poor, *Report*, C. 7684, 1895 (P.P. 1895, v. 14), pp. xxv, xxix.

endeavour . . . to make provision for his old age in accordance with his means during his working life'. The other ways by which old people might be helped were examined; endowed and other charities, C.O.S. pensions, friendly societies, Post Office savings and annuities. Of schemes for old age pensions they described over a dozen, and particularly Booth's and Chamberlain's. But they could recommend none of them; Chamberlain's they disliked for its compulsory features, Booth's because of its cost and its discouragement to thrift. They left, however, a crumb of comfort: 'we do not desire that our inquiry should preclude the consideration of any plan which may hereafter be proposed and be free from the objections which have prevented the adoption of the schemes submitted to us'.[1]

A minority report was signed by Chamberlain, Ritchie, two other members of parliament, and Charles Booth. It estimated the number of the poor among working-class people over 65 as nearly one in two, and regretted the majority's lack of any constructive policy concerning pensions. More interesting, perhaps, was the report of Henry Broadhurst, the stone-mason who had been under-secretary for Home Affairs in Gladstone's third government. He called for fundamental changes in the treatment of the aged poor: the Poor Law and charity were not sufficient. The maintenance of the aged should be a public charge upon the whole community, and should include a general scheme of pensions. 'A state of things in which two out of three of large sections of the labouring population are condemned, after lives spent in hard and ill-paid toil in the service of the whole community, to linger out the rest of their days in pauperism, demands, in my opinion, the immediate attention of Parliament.'[2] As for the cost: 'so long as four or five hundred millions sterling are every year paid in rent and interest . . . the wage-earners will

[1] *Ibid.*, p. xxxvii.   [2] *Ibid.*, p. xcviii.

be slow to believe that the provision of twenty millions for the maintenance of aged workers offers any insuperable difficulty to a willing Chancellor of the Exchequer'.[1]

Amid these shifting currents the C.O.S. stood firm. Loch's position was stated in a long paper, replete with tables, which he read to the South Wales and Monmouthshire Poor Law Conference at Brecon in May 1892; the title was 'Pauperism and Old-Age Pensions'. He pointed to the general decline of pauperism since 1834, which made the surviving pauperism of old age proportionately greater; yet the model Boards of Guardians of Bradfield and Brixworth had reduced their rates of aged pauperism almost to nothing (at Brixworth 56 per cent. of the people over 60 were paupers in 1871, 5-6 per cent. in 1891). Pension and insurance schemes were unnecessary because people could provide for themselves (for example, through friendly societies), and would do so when not led to expect help from public funds. He scouted the argument that the labourer deserved a pension from the State as the great 'Labour master' in compensation for a hard life; 'we labour for ourselves', not for the State. He dismissed the contention that a pension which all received would degrade none. Common sense had hitherto held dependence on the funds of the community to be degrading; and the evil of dependence would remain. Two paths faced his hearers, one leading to social independence, the other to dependence: which did they choose?[2]

Thomas Mackay, in *Insurance and Saving: A Report on the*

[1] R.C. on Aged Poor, *Report*, C. 7684, 1895 (P.P. 1895, v. 14), p. c.

[2] This paper was printed in the *Report of Proceedings of the South Wales and Monmouthshire Poor Law Conference, May 24-25, 1892,* and will be found in the series of reports of *Poor Law Conferences*; it is also in Bernard Bosanquet (ed.), *Aspects of the Social Problem* (1895). Loch also published a pamphlet, *Old Age Pensions and Pauperism, an Inquiry as to . . . the Statistics . . . quoted by the Rt. Hon. J. Chamberlain . . .* (1892). See also above, p. 70.

The C.O.S. and the Movement of Ideas

Existing Opportunities for Working-Class Thrift, a volume in the Charity Organisation series published by the Society and Swan Sonnenschein in 1892, took the same position. Voluntary insurance by thrift, through the friendly societies, could provide for old age; there was no need to absolve a large class from the task of supplying itself with necessities during a portion of life. 'What society requires for its reformation is not that each man when he comes to the age of 60 shall find that his fairy godmother, the State, has put a balance at his bankers, but rather that, during his life, he shall have followed the prudent course of so limiting his responsibilities to his income that at 60 he finds himself in possession, by his own exertion, of adequate provision for his old age. . . . To remove the necessity of providing for old age would be to remove one of the most potent influences of civilisation.'[1] The same arguments were repeated by Mrs Bosanquet in *The Strength of the People* in 1902. Wage-earners could provide for their old age, and did so, through the friendly societies. Even the lowest-paid wage-earner could save if he wished, because, except for the first fourteen years of his married life, his children would be doubling or trebling the family income by their own earnings; and later, they would help to support him.[2]

In its *Annual Reports* the C.O.S. also kept the faith. Grants from the State (old age pensions) would weaken social obligations: charity strengthens them. The State can act as paymaster: it cannot foster character.[3] In 1898 it deplored changing social opinion, which lowered the standard of independence, and saw no principle at stake in old age pensions but argued for them as a social right. Advocates of pensions might admit that 'acceptance of this bounty may

---

[1] *Insurance and Saving* (1892), pp. 32-3.
[2] Helen Bosanquet, *Strength of the People*, ch. 8, esp. p. 242.
[3] C.O.S., 27th *Annual Report*, 1895, p. 15.

damp the ardour of the people for the laborious processes of self-support and foresight', but set aside the argument as irrelevant.[1]

So far, the debate over old age pensions had been conducted chiefly by middle-class people. The members of the C.O.S. stood by the principle of the individual's responsibility for providing for his old age by thrift – supplemented, it might be, by a pension from the C.O.S. If he had failed in this duty, let him go to the Poor Law. Those on the other side argued from the statistics of aged pauperism, and sought means of removing a slur on the nation and an obstacle to individualism. Working people largely remained aloof, and the T.U.C. in particular.[2] This was partly because the more careful spirits belonged to the friendly societies, and these (financially unstable as many of them were)[3] preserved for working people a vested interest in the old order or lack of order; for the rest there was the Poor Law – probably outdoor relief, at worst a workhouse ward perhaps a little more comfortable than in earlier times. By the end of the century, when other official committees had reported and temporised, working-class opinion was moving toward old age pensions, and politicians were ready to support some such scheme, lest worse befall. For the moment the dykes held; but soon only the C.O.S. would be manning them.

[1] C.O.S., 30th *Annual Report*, 1898, p. 3.

[2] See the useful article by R. V. Sires, 'The Beginning of British Legislation for Old-Age Pensions,' *Journal of Economic History*, Summer, 1954, esp. pp. 240, 246-8.

[3] *Ibid.*, pp. 232, 237; Sir Arnold Wilson, *Old Age Pensions*, pp. 9, 11, 17, 25.

CHAPTER VII

The Defence of Charity, 1901-1913

As the twentieth century opened, the C.O.S. seemed outwardly as strong as ever. Its financial accounts for 1913, as for earlier years, showed its strength and solidarity. Donations and subscriptions to the Council in that year brought in £10,614; in addition there were subscriptions to several smaller funds, of which £1,898 subscribed for special cases was the largest. The expenses of the Central Office (including publications) were £5,758. The District Committee account included £2,105 granted to District Committees and £5,268 expended for District Secretaries' salaries and training expenses. The District Committees spent £10,956 on general expenses, £14,868 on pensions and £22,169 on special cases (expenditure on pensions had declined, after the introduction of Old Age Pensions, from a maximum of £20,687 in 1908). The number of cases decided by the District Committees, which was falling in 1897, continued to fall, and stood at 14,059 in 1901. It rose to 20,590 in 1906, 20,656 in 1909, but then declined again, to 18,028 in 1911 and 16,399 in 1913.[1]

There were certain changes in the staff of the Central Office. C. J. Hamilton replaced Austin Ward (who died after serving on the staff since 1894) as assistant secretary in 1906, and E. C. Price was promoted to General Assistant Secretary. In 1908 there were three other assistant secretaries, Miss Emily Simey, L. E. Buncher and R. G. Wright. Miss Marsland

[1] For earlier figures, see pp. 34-35, 95-97. Changes in the arrangement of the tables of cases handled by the District Committees make it impossible to give figures of the numbers assisted and not assisted in these later years.

The Charity Organisation Society

was also on the staff as Travelling Secretary. D. R. Sharpe was secretary to the Thrift Sub-committee, as he had been since 1905. E. S. Kemp succeeded Lieutenant-Colonel Montefiore as secretary to the Medical Sub-committee in 1906. In 1909 Hamilton held the title of Lecturer and gave a course and took part in the tutorial work of the School of Sociology.[1] In 1911 L. V. Shairpe (organising secretary of the Leeds C.O.S.) joined Miss Marsland as Travelling Secretary on a part-time basis. The Rev. J. C. Pringle (ultimately Loch's successor) first appears in the lists at the end of 1912 as an assistant secretary responsible for the Districts Sub-committee.

The Provincial Sub-committee continued its busy work of arranging visits and conducting correspondence between the C.O.S. in London and the Charity Organisation and similar societies in the provinces. Even more important, it helped to arrange for many secretaries and other members of provincial Charity Organisation societies to receive training in London, presumably in a District Office, and it also recommended London-trained persons to provincial societies.[2] 'Additional Provincial Members' were added to the Council in 1906. A winter conference was held in January 1909, in London, and thereafter two national conferences were held each year, a winter one in London and a summer one in some provincial city. In 1913 there were 135 societies in the United Kingdom which were in correspondence with the C.O.S. in London.

New District Committees were formed. Two in West Ham (North and South), outside the Metropolitan area, were started in 1908, and one for Norwood and S. Dulwich in the same year. In 1910 a separate committee came into being for

[1] 39th *Annual Report*, 1907, p. 13. Hamilton was subsequently professor of economics in Calcutta and Patna, India. (B. Webb, *Our Partnership* (1948), biographical index, p. 507.)

[2] See the annual reports of the Provincial Sub-committee in the C.O.S. *Annual Reports*.

The Defence of Charity

the City of London (previously part of the Finsbury Committee), and another was begun at Sydenham. The number of District Committees in 1913 was 42. The salaried staff assisting the District Committees grew also. In 1913 there were 19 Secretaries, 13 District Secretaries, 4 Organising Secretaries (R. Sanderson, L. F. Ellis, Miss Kelly, Miss Plater); H. L. Woollcombe was General Organising Secretary. Secretaries were paid £150 (men) and £100-£130 (women); District Secretaries £170-£200, Organising Secretaries £250 (men) and £200 (women).[1] H. V. Toynbee was Organising Secretary for Southwark, Newington, Bermondsey and N. Lambeth until 1907 when, at Loch's recommendation, he joined the staff of the Royal Commission on the Poor Laws as a special investigator to make a study of endowed and voluntary charities, and the relations between charities and the Poor Law, in a number of towns and rural parishes, particularly in the North. He was able to do yeoman service as a speaker to provincial Charity Organisation societies while engaged on his official duties in 1907, but was compelled through ill health to retire not long afterwards.

In 1905 the C.O.S. made its one and only change of headquarters, when it moved from the familiar rooms, first hired by Ribton-Turner in 1869, at 15 Buckingham Street, to Denison House, 296 Vauxhall Bridge Road, near Victoria Station. Denison House was built by a separate company under the leadership of Sir Arthur Clay with the purpose of providing offices for several charitable societies, the C.O.S. being the principal tenant. It thus represented a useful piece of 'charity organisation', and claimed to be analogous to the Societies Houses in New York and Boston. And there the C.O.S. (and its successor) have remained ever since. Denison House also provided a room for the Denison Club, a club for C.O.S. workers which had had a room previously at the top

[1] 43rd *Annual Report*, 1911, p. 26.

of 15 Buckingham Street. It had been started in 1885. It held meetings at which papers were read, and served also as a place for sociability, especially at tea after meetings of the Council. Its room was open on weekdays from 12 to 8.[1]

In many other ways the C.O.S. was taking stock of itself and of charity in these years. Loch read a paper before the Council in 1903 on *The Development of Charity Organisation.* He reminded his hearers that the Society's object was the improvement of the condition of the poor. 'Always it has laid stress on the view that the condition of the poor could not be improved unless assistance were turned to account so as to strengthen character. . . . Relief, we would argue, as commonly given, tends to weaken the whole circle of reciprocal obligations of which for most of us the family is the centre.' Now socialism was challenging this position, since it proposed to provide security and maintenance for the working classes out of the taxable resources of the community.

Loch's proposals for the future (apart from better attendance by representatives of the District Committees at Council meetings and less preoccupation with the routines of casework) were of two sorts. For the Society he wished the District Committees to become more representative, drawing in more local people, including members of the working class; he thought each Committee might have a Conference Secretary, and become or join a Joint Committee for the district. Such a committee would work for measures of improvement in the district: enforcement of the sanitary laws against overcrowding, physical training for school children, a system of apprenticeship, a co-operative plan for giving advice concerning the rearing and upbringing of young children, better methods of industrial remuneration,

[1] *Charity Organisation Review,* September 1901; H. Bosanquet, *Social Work in London,* p. 77.

such as co-partnership, and the separate payment of the rates (Loch disliked the practice of the landlord compounding the rates with the rent, since this bred irresponsibility in the tenants regarding local government expenditure).

Loch's other proposals related to the Poor Law, and foreshadowed the ideas of the Majority Report of the Royal Commission on the Poor Laws of 1909. He wanted the Poor Law authorty to be a committee of the borough council; the Guardians and the separate poor rate (which implied the right of the individual to be supported by it) should be abolished. He wanted the voluntary and endowed charities to be recognised by the State as part of the organisation of relief: they would co-operate with the local Poor Law authority, and would be responsible for helping most of the people hitherto given outdoor relief; outdoor relief and allowances, particularly widows' allowances, would cease. There should be an improved system of inquiry, record, verification of cases; relieving officers should be given appropriate training.[1]

These ideas were far from new in Loch's mind. In a Christmas letter to an American friend, Miss Morse, in 1893, he had sketched a similar plan. Outdoor relief would be the responsibility of the endowed charities and voluntary societies in each parish, working under a board, and the Poor Law would be left (except for emergency cases) with responsibility for indoor relief only, organised on a county basis. In this way he hoped to provide for the aged without a system of public pensions.[2]

As far as charitable societies were concerned, Loch's hopes

---

[1] C. S. Loch, *The Development of Charity Organisation*, June 1, 1903. Private and Confidential. For Members of the District Committees of the C.O.S. (In bound volume, 'Pamphlets. C. S. Loch', in C.O.S. library.) This is the paper referred to by Mrs Bosanquet, *Social Work in London*, p. 88.

[2] Letter in possession of Mrs R. B. Mowat.

for greater co-operation among them seemed to be coming nearer to fulfilment. A new movement which the C.O.S. accepted as a friend rather than a rival was the Guild of Help movement, which began in Bradford in 1905. Guilds of Help were started in several places, especially in the North: Sheffield, Halifax, Manchester, Leeds, Warrington, Newcastle, Bolton; also in Bristol, Plymouth, Birmingham, Croydon. By 1910 some 60 were in existence. Their aim was to impart a civic character to charitable work, to bring together citizens of all classes, and to co-operate with the Poor Law, public health and education authorities. They made use of voluntary visitors serving under a district head, and combined friendly visiting with the giving of help to those in need. Their aims included the prevention of overlapping and waste in charity, and the bringing of lasting improvement in each case where help was given – objects entirely consistent with the C.O.S. philosophy.[1] The Provincial Sub-committee of the C.O.S. welcomed them, and invited them to the C.O.S. summer conference at Leeds in 1910: ten sent delegates, and others 'were represented informally or acknowledged the invitation in a friendly spirit'.[2] Two Guilds of Help (Falmouth, Middlesbrough) joined the list of corresponding societies of the C.O.S. A few other societies on this list bore names other than 'C.O.S.' – for example, Civic League, Social Service League – and in some instances this represented a fusion of a local C.O.S. with another society. In 1910 the Bristol C.O.S. amalgamated with the Bristol Civic League of Personal Service under the name of the Bristol Civic League.

Another newcomer was the Personal Service Association, founded in the winter of 1908-09. Its object was to promote

[1] C. Osborn, 'The Guild of Help Movement,' *C.O. Review*, June 1910.
[2] 42nd *Annual Report*, 1910, p. 58.

friendly visiting, and some of the C.O.S. District Committees welcomed persons supplied by it to the roster of their voluntary workers (though this, of course, added to the number of people needing training).[1] Referring to these and other visitors, including Health Visitors (nurses employed in several towns under the Medical Officer of Health to promote infant welfare),[2] the 40th *Annual Report* of the Council (for 1908) hopefully remarked that 'the value of visiting . . . has reasserted itself, and more than ever has the home become the object of charitable intervention. The widespread desire to introduce some system like the Elberfeld system has helped to promote this, but chiefly and above all it is due to science – the science of separate departments of social work, medicine and sanitation for instance, and no less the science of charity.'[3]

A much larger movement for co-operation in charity – charity organisation in the original sense of the C.O.S.'s use of the term – was that of registration in London: the keeping of a number of District Registers in which many co-operating charities registered their cases. In part it was linked with parochial committees which, under clerical leadership, were being formed to administer parochial relief on C.O.S. lines; there were twelve such committees co-operating with the C.O.S. in 1910.[4] Larger local councils of welfare agencies, public and private, were also being formed. The Stepney Council of Public Welfare, with which three local District Committees co-operated, dated from 1906.[5]

In 1909 registration schemes were in force in Chelsea, Hampstead, Marylebone, S. St Pancras, Shoreditch, Upper Holloway; that at Chelsea was four years old. The Marylebone

[1] 40th *Annual Report*, 1908, p. 18; 41st, p. 32.
[2] S. and B. Webb, *The State and the Doctor* (1910), pp. 177-85.
[3] 40th *Annual Report*, p. 18.
[4] 41st *Annual Report*, pp. 12-13.
[5] 39th *Annual Report*, 1907, pp. 8-9.

register was the joint responsibility of the C.O.S. District Committee and the Church Army; the St Pancras register was started by the District Committee; the other registers were apparently kept by *ad hoc* bodies with which the District Committees co-operated. At Hampstead registration was part of the work of the Council of Social Welfare, in which the local District Committee was merged: the General Executive Committee, elected triennially by the Council (consisting of 134 representatives of different societies and institutions), served also as the C.O.S. District Committee although it was responsible to other organisations than the C.O.S. – a situation which strained the 'liberal tolerance' of the Council of the C.O.S.[1] T. Hancock Nunn was the moving spirit in this experiment.[2]

The movement for registration grew rapidly. It was not confined to London; indeed 37 of the provincial Charity Organisation societies had registration schemes in 1911, several of them of some years standing. In London a Conference of Honorary Registrars was held on February 18, 1909, and a month later the Administrative Committee of the Council of the C.O.S. authorised the establishment of a Central Registry at the Central Office. By February 1911 there were 29 District Registries 'worked either as part of the (C.O.S.) District Committee organisation, or in close co-operation with it'. These received reports from 1,150 agencies – Boards of Guardians, churches, missions, charitable societies, School Care Committees, health societies – and had accumulated over 130,000 names. Some District Registries sent out as many as 300 reports per month. The Central Registry received reports from 58 hospitals and other general organisations (whose cases did not originate locally in the districts),

---

[1] 40th *Annual Report*, 1908 (presented April 28, 1909), pp. 12-16.
[2] See Loch's comments, ' "A Social Democracy" and "Social Welfare" ', *C.O. Review*, June 1910.

The Defence of Charity

at the rate of over 2,000 a month, and by 1911 had stored some 21,000 entries.[1] In 1912, however, the Central Registry stopped indexing the cases it was notified of, and simply transmitted them to the appropriate District Registries.

In 1911, by a resolution of the Administrative Committee on February 23, the Provincial Registration Committee was established to replace, though not completely to supersede, the Conference of Registrars (which had met 16 times in 1909-10 and continued to meet from time to time). The report of the Committee for 1913 recorded that 1,612 agencies were co-operating with the 37 District Registries then at work, and 118 agencies were sending their notifications (totalling 57,616) to the Central Registry. The work of the District Registries can be gauged from the figures which follow:[2]

	1911	1912	1913
Names received	170,000 *	257,982	268,852
Reports sent out	35,000 *	48,931	42,628

* Estimate for year based on 9 months' figures.

These figures are a remarkable testimony to the progress of co-operation in charity, and to the volume of work carried on by voluntary bodies at this stage in the history of the C.O.S. – before the war and the great increase in the welfare work of the State.

A proposal of a different character, which the C.O.S. could not support, came to a head in the winter of 1909-10. An Association of Subscribers to Charities was started in the City of London in 1907 as an outgrowth of a rather anomalous committee of the C.O.S. for the City. Its object was to

[1] Report of the Central Registrar on Registration of Assistance, in 42nd *Annual Report*, pp. 74-7.

[2] Report of the Provisional Registration Committee for the year 1913, in 45th *Annual Report* pp. 66-9.

promote co-operation between the charities of London, including those outside the City. It raised money which it spent on relief. Becoming ambitious, its leaders, who included A. H. Paterson, formerly an Organising Secretary of the C.O.S., promoted a larger body, the London Association of Social Welfare, into which the Association of Subscribers was to merge. It proposed to form a Central Association and in each borough a council whose task would be to promote co-operation between public and private relief agencies and social and industrial undertakings. It would thus parallel the work of the C.O.S., and it is not surprising that the Council voted to take no part in it.[1]

There was something it could less easily ignore: the rising tide of State intervention in social welfare. Here too, however, the situation was far from hopeless in the Society's view. For we must notice that some of the social legislation early in the century not only recognised but demanded the co-operation of voluntary workers and societies with the new public agencies. For example, under the Education (Provision of Meals) Act, 1906, the London County Council organised Children's Care Committees (of private persons) in 1907 – though the L.C.C. did not at first provide school meals. Skilled Apprenticeship Committees (to help school leavers) were formed with the same composition and sponsorship. The C.O.S. co-operated with these new bodies, though with some uneasiness. As the 40th *Annual Report* observed:

> It will be noticed how heavy is the burthen that the State is placing upon its citizens in the execution of these new laws. If voluntary helpers do not come forward in large

[1] 41st *Annual Report*, 1909, pp. 20-6; 42nd, p. 5. For an earlier scheme for a new organisation in which the C.O.S. was invited to merge itself see the correspondence between Loch and H. Burdett over Burdett's 'Pandenominational' scheme, *C.O. Review*, November 1895.

numbers to fulfil the obligations which the State imposes, there can be but one alternative, that these departments will be managed by officials, and must almost inevitably lose most of the characteristics that will make them useful to society.

Another instance of this was the Unemployed Workmen Act of 1905. This measure, part socialist, part individualist (in so far as it relied on charity), was enacted by the Conservatives at the instance of Walter Long and Gerald Balfour, successive presidents of the Local Government Board. Its immediate cause was another Mansion House Fund and the proposals of a Mansion House Committee of 1903 which so impressed Long that he improvised for London in 1904 the machinery later provided in the Act. The object was to help relieve the unemployed outside the Poor Law and without disfranchisement; for this purpose a Central Unemployed Body and local Distress Committees were created for London, and Distress Committees in the larger towns. These Committees were to include borough councillors, Poor Law Guardians, and persons experienced in the relief of distress (i.e. representatives of charitable bodies). The Distress Committees received funds from the rates only to provide labour registers (forerunners of the Labour Exchanges of 1909) and to assist emigration and migration within the country – powers very little used. Funds for relief works were to come from subscriptions from the charitable public and from the municipalities; after 1906 help from a special grant made by Parliament to the Local Government Board was available as well.[1]

The Central Unemployed Body for London operated a farm colony for unemployed men at Hollesley Bay. Relief works of the usual sort (paving, sewering and the like) were

[1] S. and B. Webb, *English Poor Law History*, II, ii, 649-60; W. H. Beveridge, *Unemployment: A Problem of Industry*, pp. 159-91.

The Charity Organisation Society

provided by many municipal authorities. The policy was, in fact, an elaboration of Chamberlain's circular of March 1886 and reflected a belief in the value of relief works which the experience of the intervening years did little to justify. In spite of its recognition of charity, the Unemployed Workmen Act was received by the C.O.S. with scepticism. Relief work, the C.O.S. believed, was harmful, both for the good workman and the bad; for the former because it debased his skill and put him in bad company, for the latter because it encouraged him in improvidence.[1] In West Ham it co-operated with the Distress Committee in the winter of 1905-1906, and supplied a large staff to investigate all applicants. 4,199 cases were examined; 56·2 per cent. were found eligible for help, 43·8 per cent. ineligible ('the man who does not, cannot, or will not work', 19·8 per cent., unclassed, 24 per cent.). Yet only a few of the 2,359 applicants judged eligible could, in fact, be given work.[2]

Already, in November 1904, the Council had issued the report of a Special Committee on the Relief of Distress from Want of Employment. Fifteen persons, seven of them Guardians, served, including W. A. Bailward, Sir William Chance, Sir Arthur Clay, the Bishop of Islington (C. H. Turner), George Lansbury (who attended the hearings frequently), H. G. Willink, W. Vallance, previously Clerk to the Whitechapel Guardians, and Thomas Mackay. Evidence, chiefly from C.O.S. District Secretaries, was given for several districts, and the experience of municipal relief works was recounted. The report observed that there had been a large increase in pauperism in London, due to 'altered administration'; that several Unions (Poplar, Camberwell, Bermondsey, West Ham) gave outdoor relief without the workhouse test. Worse, public opinion had changed. 'The

[1] See above, pp. 131-36; also discussion in 37th *Annual Report*, 1905, pp. 5-11. [2] *Ibid.*, p. 12. Cf. 38th *Report*

The Defence of Charity

Poor Law is converted practically into an enormously rich rate-endowed public charity open to all-comers. . . . And as the theory gains ground that want of work must be met through public authorities by the direct provision of employment, the Borough Council takes the place of the Poor Law as the centre for organising employment-relief.' Later it observed: 'Now there is a widespread opinion that relief under these circumstances [private charity to 'thrifty and careful people'] is an indignity and that work at a wage should in all cases be available and should be offered.'[1] George Lansbury wanted work to be provided, but by the Guardians, not by the borough councils, in workshops and farm colonies. He opposed the giving of a dole without work: 'I really object to the giving of money for nothing.'[2]

In its conclusions, the Report reiterated the earlier advice of the C.O.S. The unemployed should be in the care of joint public – voluntary committees, which would investigate all applicants, relieving those of good character by charity, and referring the rest to the Poor Law. It opposed the offer of work-relief without disfranchisement: 'it represents the acceptance on the part of the State of an obligation to provide employment-relief practically to all-comers'. This would prevent labour mobility and lead to a new serfdom. Once again, urging the importance of forethought and thrift, it declared: 'it is clear that the problem is only in part industrial and economic. In great part it is a problem of social competence and moral responsibility.'[3]

Four years later the C.O.S. issued another report, on Unskilled Labour. It owed much to the labours of W. H. Beveridge, who served at first as its secretary and who had already begun those studies which led to his classic work, *Unemployment*, in 1909; the hearings of the special com-

[1] C.O.S., *The Relief of Distress from Want of Employment*, 1904, pp. 18, 22. [2] *Ibid.*, pp. 33, 161. [3] *Ibid.*, pp. 49, 50.

· 157 ·

mittee responsible for the report took place between October 1905 and January 1906. It examined the extent, character and effects of casual labour, especially in the London docks. It recommended decasualisation, public labour exchanges, the training of children leaving the elementary schools in occupations offering permanent employment, and the encouragement of societies for mutual thrift on the principles of insurance. It referred to German schemes of voluntary unemployment insurance. Local relief works and back-to-the-land schemes it believed to be harmful or of little value.[1]

In the Old Age Pensions Act of 1908 the government embarked on a new policy; for it was a piece of social legislation for the welfare of the poor which did not call for the co-operation of charity. In addition, it gave little encouragement – rather the reverse – to thrift and providence and individual responsibility. Cutting through the previous arguments over voluntary and contributory schemes for pensions, it provided for non-contributory pensions to persons reaching the age of 70, subject to a means test. Those who had at any time received Poor Law relief were disqualified (this disqualification lapsed at the end of 1910), as were ex-prisoners and those who had failed to work according to their abilities, opportunities and needs for the maintenance of themselves and their dependents. This last provision, a gesture towards the encouragement of thrift and industry which it was hard to enforce in practice, allowed payments into a friendly society up to the age of 60 to count as proof of non-disqualification on this score. Old age pensioners were not, as such, to be disfranchised.[2]

The C.O.S. had never given up the fight against old age pensions. In 1900 a Committee on Old Age Pensions had been formed with headquarters at 15 Buckingham Street. W. A.

[1] C.O.S., *Special Committee on Unskilled Labour Report*, 1908.
[2] Sir Arnold Wilson, *Old Age Pensions*, pp. 40-7.

Bailward was honorary secretary and Sir William Chance honorary treasurer; Loch, Bousfield, Fitch, Mackay and several other C.O.S. leaders were members. In 1903 it republished in book form several papers, mostly written by Loch and Bailward, criticising the various pension schemes of the time, and describing foreign experience.[1] The Act of 1908 contained nothing to commend itself to the C.O.S. The Society deplored it as thoughtless action, taken without adequate discussion and without the elaborate planning which had preceded the old age insurance scheme in Germany. It discouraged thrift. It would not relieve the suffering of the poor, but would simply give added comforts to those who were not in need and be a substitute for pensions, 'hitherto provided from a voluntary sense of obligation by employers and landowners'. It created a new class of dependents on the State – as did the provision of school meals and work-relief. 'Old Age Pensions . . . will give the idea that the country will eventually provide for all necessities.'[2] The pensions previously arranged by the C.O.S. did not cease. District Committees continued to visit and help their pensioners, in the belief that the old age pension of 5s. a week needed supplementing for those who were deserving and lacked any other means.[3]

*　　*　　*　　*　　*

Meanwhile, Loch and several other leaders of the C.O.S. were involved in the long-drawn-out deliberations of the Royal Commission on the Poor Laws and Relief of Distress, which had been appointed by the outgoing Conservative government late in 1905. This grand inquest into the working

[1] *Old-Age Pensions: the Case against Old-Age Pension Schemes: A Collection of Short Papers* (Macmillan, 1903).

[2] 'The Old Age Pensions Scheme', *C.O. Review*, September 1908; C.O.S., 40th *Annual Report*, p. 2.

[3] 40th *Report*, p. 6.

of the Poor Law as it had been shaped after the report of the commission of 1832 was not the product of any public agitation but was, none the less, a logical development from the recent and largely haphazard changes in policy regarding the relief of the aged, the sick and, above all, the able-bodied unemployed. And in its composition the Commission bore striking testimony to the high public standing of the C.O.S. at this time, for no less than six of its nineteen members were prominent figures in the C.O.S.: Loch, Mrs Bosanquet, Octavia Hill, the Rev. L. R. Phelps, T. Hancock Nunn, and the Rev. Thory Gage Gardiner. Other members included Charles Booth, Mrs Webb, George Lansbury; the chairman was Lord George Hamilton.[1]

Loch played a large part in the work of the Royal Commission. He prepared a memorandum on the old Poor Law before 1834. He was chairman of a sub-committee which reported on the principles on which outdoor relief should be given. He inspired two of the special investigations which the Commission undertook: on the overlapping of the work of the voluntary hospitals and the medical relief of the Poor Law, and on the relations between the Poor Law and charity in representative towns and rural areas. Two men connected with the staff of the C.O.S., H. V. Toynbee and the Rev. J. C. Pringle, served the Commission as investigators. Mrs Bosanquet set two other inquiries going: into outdoor relief in Bermondsey and the effect of outdoor relief on women's wages.[2]

The Majority Report (which all the C.O.S. members

[1] The Rev. L. R. Phelps, Provost of Oriel College, Oxford, was for many years chairman of the Oxford Board of Guardians of the Poor. The Rev. T. Gage Gardiner was rector of St George the Martyr, Southwark.

[2] S. and B. Webb, *English Poor Law History*, II, ii, 506; for Mrs Webb's rather unkind references to Loch's part in the sittings of the Commission, *ibid.*, p. 494, and her *Our Partnership* (1948), pp. 341, 343, 357-8, 377, 389, 420.

The Defence of Charity

signed) represented substantially the C.O.S. point of view, though with several modifications. It recommended the abolition of the Guardians and the transference of the administration of the Poor Law (to be renamed Public Assistance) to the county and county borough councils. It recommended more specialised provision for old people, children and the able-bodied unemployed. Old people should receive adequate outdoor relief, or if needing institutional care should be in small homes. Children should be boarded out or kept at home (e.g. by outdoor relief at a sufficient rate to a widowed mother); on the other hand school meals should be provided, where needed, by the Poor Law rather than by the education authority. Unemployment should be prevented by decasualisation, discouragement of blind-alley jobs, raising the school leaving age to 15, labour exchanges and the postponement of public works as much as possible to slack times. Relief of the unemployed should remain the responsibility of the Poor Law, but should be restorative and discriminating: for decent working men (if not helped by a voluntary aid committee) in industrial institutions (perhaps making use of disused workhouses) or in agricultural colonies, for loafers in detention colonies under the Home Office. Unemployment insurance and invalidity insurance (for early superannuation) were recommended. Medical care should be provided through provident dispensaries; a 'gratuitous medical service' was rejected except for paupers. Disfranchisement should not apply to those who received medical relief nor to anyone who was in receipt of other relief for less than three months in a year. In general, the reformed Poor Law of the Majority would abandon the ideas of deterrence and 'less eligibility'; one of its main principles was that help should be 'preventive, curative and restorative.'[1]

[1] R.C. on Poor Laws, *Majority Report*, Part IX, para. 71 (octavo ed. vol. II, p. 215).

On two large points these proposals differed from those of the Minority Report signed by Mrs Webb, Lansbury and two other members of the Commission. The Majority favoured co-operation between charitable and voluntary bodies and the Poor Law. Medical relief was to be organised under local Medical Assistance Committees representing the Poor Law, the doctors, hospitals and friendly societies. For general purposes Voluntary Aid Committees were to be formed, representing the Poor Law, charitable societies and trusts, the clergy, friendly societies; these were to handle most applications for outdoor relief, including cases referred by the Poor Law. They would have been, if they had ever come into being, the equivalent of District Committees of the C.O.S. on an official basis.

Secondly, the Majority Report retained the Poor Law, in fact though not in name, though it would have relieved it of much of its load. It did so chiefly because it testified, like the C.O.S., to the importance of the family and the individual – who, in the Minority's proposals, were in danger of being shuttled backwards and forwards between the several specialised services which it envisaged. The Majority also doubted whether authorities with quite different primary purposes could be entrusted with the care of those who had lost their economic independence.

By contrast, the Minority demanded the abolition of the 'general mixed workhouse' and the break-up of the Poor Law. The duties of the Poor Law were to be divided among a number of functional services: a birth and infancy service, a children's authority, a unified medical service on public health lines, a Ministry of Labour with labour exchanges, industrial training centres and detention colonies for the unemployed. Non-compulsory unemployment insurance was recommended, compulsory health insurance rejected. The only comprehensive relief agency which was to survive

The Defence of Charity

was a Registrar of Public Assistance in each district, who among other things was to manage a 'small and strictly temporary Receiving House' for 'Omitted Cases'. The Majority's Voluntary Aid Committees were sternly criticised as 'irresponsible Committees of benevolent amateurs', designed to withdraw relief from popular control.[1]

The two Reports were issued early in 1909 and had, particularly the Majority Report, a very good reception. The main proposals of both were, however, ignored by the government. There was no immediate 'break-up' of the Poor Law, no abolition of the Guardians, no erasing of the old name. The government, occupied as it was with the controversy over the Budget of 1909, the Parliament Bill, the Ulster crisis and other troubles of the times, was not ready for so large and contentious a reform, and turned instead to the schemes of health and unemployment insurance and the establishment of labour exchanges which were pressed by Lloyd George and Winston Churchill. A unanimous report might conceivably have fared better. The Webbs, however, not content with having prevented unanimity, began the large and highly organised campaign of the National Committee for the Break-up of the Poor Law which they formed. Their purpose, disregarding the similarities between the two reports, was 'to commit the country to a policy of complete communal responsibility for the fact of destitution'. Their achievement was to alienate the government, bore the public and postpone reform.

[1] Royal Commission on the Poor Laws and Relief of Distress, *Minority Report*, Cd. 4499, 1909, p. 394 (octavo edition). The Reports were issued in a folio edition (one large volume containing Majority and Minority Reports), and in an octavo edition (vols. I and II are the Majority Report, vol. III the Minority). The Webbs also published an edition of the Minority Report. For an excellent and stimulating discussion of the two reports see Una Cormack, *The Welfare State: the Royal Commission on the Poor Laws, 1905-1909, and the Welfare State*, Loch Memorial Lecture, 1953, Family Welfare Association.

The Charity Organisation Society

The Majority Report remains of interest as the ultimate embodiment of the idea of charity organisation as preached and practised by the C.O.S. It contained the proposals sketched by Loch in 1893 and 1903: a reorganised Poor Law for indoor relief, statutory co-operation between public and charitable bodies for outdoor relief; it even proposed to return school meals to the responsibility of the Poor Law. It exalted charity; indeed, part VII, on 'Charities and the Relief of Distress', contained 'a good deal of me', as Loch wrote to a friend.[1] It did more, it registered the progress of moderate opinion, including C.O.S. opinion, on poverty and its relief. It gave the quietus to ideas of 'less eligibility', of the iniquity of outdoor relief; it reduced the emphasis on the deterrent character of public assistance. In some ways it went beyond C.O.S. opinion, for example in its attitude to public works and to disfranchisement. Three members of the Society added reservations to their signatures in the Report: Loch and Mrs Bosanquet concerning work-relief for the unemployed, Octavia Hill on the proposals for medical relief and the retreat from disfranchisement.

In the Council there was a good deal of opposition to the Majority Report. After several special meetings, at which Loch read papers on different aspects of it, the Council resolved unanimously in December 1909 that, though it was not in complete agreement with it, it believed that reform of the Poor Law lay rather along the lines of the Majority Report than of the Minority; and that the Society should not restrain its members in advocating or criticising it.[2] Loch himself gave many addresses up and down the country in favour of the Majority Report.

[1] Letter to Miss Morse, December 25, 1909.
[2] C.O.S. 41st *Annual Report*, 1909, p. 4. Loch gave his views in the *C.O. Review*, February 1909; later issues in 1909 and in March and April 1910 have other articles on the Majority and Minority Reports.

The Defence of Charity

Ultimately, the Majority Report had little influence on social policy. True, the Poor Law was renamed Public Assistance and transferred to committees of the county and county borough councils in 1929. The co-operation recommended between public authority and charity never became official policy; the Voluntary Aid and Medical Assistance committees never came into being. Nor, on the other hand, was the Minority Report much more influential. The Poor Law was not so much broken up as eroded in the next generation: by war, depression, unemployment, contributory pensions, maternity and child welfare legislation. The Welfare State was constructed partially and piecemeal between 1914 and 1945, then completed and put in order in 1948. At that time the Poor Law was nationalised under the name of National Assistance, and confined chiefly to what had previously been outdoor relief; and compulsory and universal National Insurance came to provide for the old, the sick and the unemployed, assisted by the National Health Service and various agencies of the local authorities. This was certainly not what the Majority would have liked; neither was it quite what the Minority had proposed. The evolution of the Welfare State owed little to either, and much to the force of later circumstances. But that is another story.

The beginning of that story – the building, on empirical lines, of the Welfare State – was the National Insurance Act 1911. It satisfied neither the Majority nor the Minority. Its limited provision for unemployment insurance attracted little attention; but Part I of the Act, establishing compulsory contributory national health insurance for most classes of wage-earners, and operated largely through the friendly societies, was a different matter. Loch published a long criticism of it 'approved by the Council'. He examined the German experience with sickness insurance, which (so he claimed) increased sickness and malingering; easy-going

M · 165 ·

administration (strictness being sapped by 'kindly feeling', *Wohlwollen*), swelled the cost of the scheme. The government's scheme was equally dangerous. Its financial cost would be very high and had not been properly estimated. Its effects on the system of medical remuneration, on the hospitals and friendly societies, would be serious. It pushed to the limit the element of compulsion in the provision of medical relief, and embraced far too many people, instead of being limited to those who could not afford to save or pay for doctors' services on their own responsibility. Worst of all, it would, as German experience showed, become 'a system of public benevolence under the semblance of insurance'; it would lead to a decline in 'our sense and appreciation of social manliness and independence'. 'If we have sick insurance we must be prepared to pay for it, not only in money, but in the metal that makes the strength of men and women.'[1]

*　　*　　*　　*　　*

Already the C.O.S. was reconsidering its work in the changing circumstances of the time. W. A. Bailward, in a retrospective article on the C.O.S. in the *Quarterly Review* for January 1907, had admitted that the Society could never be popular, because of its 'necessary advocacy of economic principles' in holding 'a brief for the independence of the poor'. He lamented that it had 'fallen to some extent under a ban because it has been unable to accept the modern doctrines of State socialism'. It needed new blood, but the young men coming to London from Oxford or Cambridge with an interest in social work no longer joined the C.O.S. as a matter of course, as their predecessors had done, but considered its teachings 'antiquated and obsolete'.[2]

[1] C. S. Loch, *The National Insurance Bill: A Paper* (1911), esp. pp. 21, 25; cf. *Charity Organisation Review*, August, November, 1911.

[2] W. A. Bailward, 'The Charity Organisation Society', *Quarterly Review*, 206 (1907), 74-6.

The Defence of Charity

In 1912 Violet Markham, already known for her work as a
Guardian of the Poor Law and leader in the Civic Guild in
Chesterfield, voiced the same sort of criticism which Bailward
had deplored; and she represented just the kind of new blood
which the C.O.S. needed. She agreed that in its work of
relief and its insistence on casework, self-respect and the
importance of the family, 'its principles are on a rock'; but
she charged that in standing for the extreme individualistic
view of the causes and cure of poverty it ignored the opposite
point of view, that poverty is of social creation and that the
remedy must therefore be collective. The State exists to give
expression to the good life for the individual: it can be
creative and not, as the C.O.S. seemed to think, merely
repressive. The Society ought not to oppose all State interference in social questions, and resist every scheme of social
reform which the Liberals put forward; it should attempt to
reconcile the two views and find a middle ground between
individualism and socialism. At present it was simply out of
touch with the greatest need of the times, 'to restate the
whole of our social formulae in the light of new conditions
and new experience'. Bailward was deputed to reply. He
could only say that the C.O.S. did not oppose all State action
(for example, it favoured housing and sanitary reforms and
better provision for the feeble-minded) and was not blind to
the economic causes of poverty.[1]

In fact, the C.O.S. had conducted another self-examination
in 1909. Loch, in another address on November 18, 1907, had
warned the Council that the new tendencies in social reform
posed the question what the Society's future course should

[1] *Charity Organisation Review*, March 1912 (letter of V. Markham,
January 30 and February 14, and of Bailward, February 7; the
exchange followed a letter of Miss Markham to the *Spectator*, January
20, to which Loch replies in the February 10 issue). Cf. Una Cormack,
The Welfare State, pp. 26-9, on the C.O.S.'s 'lamentable social
failure'.

be. A Special Committee on the Organisation and Methods of the Society was appointed. Its twenty members (Loch was secretary) included Francis Morris as chairman and such veterans as Bailward, Crowder, N. Masterman, besides newer members such as the Hon. Gertrude Lubbock and Hancock Nunn. It heard evidence from 38 members between May and July 1908, but its report and evidence, running to over 400 pages, was not printed until the summer of 1909.

The report dealt with three main subjects. (1) The Society's unpopularity was examined. Witnesses mentioned as reasons the fact that many C.O.S. workers came from outside the districts in which they served, that nonconformists disliked the Society, that borough councillors were prejudiced against it (H. V. Toynbee); that its name was disliked; that it did not give enough; that its pronouncements always favoured individualism as opposed to socialism in social policy. The Rev. C. Baumgarten of the South West Ham Committee declared: 'influential people among the working class look upon the society as being largely representative of a class which they feel to be injuring them and doing them a great injustice'. Canon Barnett in a memorandum advised the Council 'for a time [to be] silent as to principles of the C.O.S.', and to devote itself 'to fostering the enthusiasm of its local committees'. The committee's recommendation was that the Society should stick to its principles but should not make pronouncements on public policy until the Administrative Committee had canvassed the District Committees for their opinions and the matter had been discussed in Council after fourteen days' notice. It also proposed that the long and seldom-used title of the Society, for Organising Charitable Relief and Repressing Mendicity, be changed to 'for Organising Charity and Improving the Condition of the Poor'.[1]

[1] The change was made in 1910, the full title of the C.O.S. becoming the Society for the Organisation of Charitable Effort and the Im-

(2) The Committee examined once more the relations of the Council and the District Committees, and co-operation with other local charities. It recommended the use of Organising Secretaries attached to groups of District Committees with the task of promoting councils of social welfare or similar co-operative bodies. The Organising Secretaries were also to promote training, visiting, registration and to arrange meetings; they were to report half-yearly to the Secretary to the Council. A Travelling Secretary should be appointed to visit the District Committees frequently. Paid secretaries of District Committees, as well as the District Secretaries and higher officials, should in future be appointed by the Council, after selection by the Administrative Committee.

(3) The work of the Council was studied. The Council was criticised for acting without the knowledge of the District Committees, and for leaving too much discretion to the Administrative Committee. Proposals for improvement included fuller agenda for Council meetings, the circulation of explanatory memoranda to District Committees, the enlargement of the number of 'additional members' of the Council from one quarter to one-third of the District Committee representatives (to bring in members of the L.C.C., borough councillors, Guardians, employers and workmen), and the requirement that one representative of each District Committee on the Council be a man.[1]

Thus the C.O.S. stood firmly by its principles and its

provement of the Condition of the Poor (H. Bosanquet, *Social Work in London*, p. 97). However, the Annual Reports from 1911 onwards simply give the Charity Organisation Society as the name of the C.O.S. and the longer title appears only as a heading for the Society's Object and Aims.

[1] *Report of the Special Committee on the Organisation and Methods of the Society.* Private and Confidential. For the use of members of Council and members of the District Committees of the Society ONLY (1909).

method. Regarding the change of its long title subscribers were told that 'those who have worked for it, contributed to its funds and given their support . . . may feel assured that on the promotion of this policy of independence the Society takes its stand, and that, come weal or woe, popularity or unpopularity, it will not abandon this policy for one of mere neutral and indeterminate co-operativeness'.[1] Commenting two years later on the National Insurance Act, Loch wrote:

> The great changes in national policy which this legislation entails imply a serious change of opinion in regard to social principles. The fear of moral injury which State dependence may cause is decreasing, and with it the dislike to receiving State aid. . . . On the other hand, the change is in some ways a sign of advance. In certain branches of work it represents a desire for a more discriminative and preventive treatment of distress (for example, in the care of mothers and children, investigation into the causes of disease, insanity, addiction to drink).
>
> This line of thought . . . involves a social revolution. It tends to place the obligations for social advance on the State, and to assume that the State is a far-seeing ruler, able to guide and manage the people in multitudinous private arrangements, as well as in public matters, and possesses the resources and the wisdom necessary for the solution of such an intricate problem.[2]

Rather than accept this, Loch proposed 'a new step – new, and yet not altogether new' in 1912. This was that the District Committees take the initiative in working for the improvement of 'bad local conditions and bad areas' in their districts. This was to urge the District Committees to undertake some of the general work for the improvement of the condition of the poor which the Council had hitherto taken the main responsibility for. Loch pointed to the existence of

[1] 41st *Annual Report*, 1909, p. 10.
[2] 43rd *Annual Report*, 1911, pp. 2-3.

areas where vice, drunkenness, gambling were more prevalent than elsewhere, to districts where overcrowding, high infant mortality, high death rate from phthisis were signs of bad conditions which dragged the people down. Octavia Hill had shown one way to tackle such conditions. The Council unanimously supported this proposal.[1]

In the same year the C.O.S. experienced a setback. The School of Sociology, in which it had much interest though no direct responsibility, was unable to raise sufficient funds for its continuance and expansion. It therefore accepted the proposal of the London School of Economics to merge itself with the School as the Department of Social Science and Administration. The Department was to be under Urwick, the head of the School of Sociology, and for two years there were to be no changes in the staff and programme of work. The change went into effect at the end of July 1912.[2]

All might have been well had the two parties to the merger been of equal weight and similar outlook. The London School of Economics was, however, a much larger institution than the School of Sociology, and was thought to be strongly coloured by the socialist views of its founders, the Webbs. Its approach to training for social work was much more theoretical than that of the School of Sociology and the C.O.S., and this inevitably influenced the work of the new department; and there was also some lack of sympathy with voluntary, charitable work.

The first generation of leaders of the C.O.S. was by now growing thin, though the public standing of the Society remained impressive. The death of Octavia Hill in 1912 removed not only one of its earliest supporters but one of its

[1] C. S. Loch, 'A Further Development', *C.O. Review*, December 1912; reprinted in *A Great Ideal and Its Champion*, pp. 197-208. This is an excellent expression of Loch's ideas and style in their latest form.

[2] 44th *Annual Report*, 1912, pp. 33-4; Marjorie J. Smith, *Professional Education for Social Work in Britain*, pp. 38-43.

staunchest and most distinguished friends. Loch had been honoured by the presentation of his portrait, by Sargent, to the Society in 1900 as a mark of his 25 years' service as secretary; it hangs in the Committee Room in Denison House. He was presented with a second and less formal portrait which Sargent also painted.[1] In 1905 his old university, Oxford, made him a Doctor of Civil Law. In February 1913 the Society held a Conversazione at the Royal Institute of Painters, attended by 700 people, at which the Archbishop of Canterbury spoke.

It was one of Loch's last public appearances. In the summer of 1913 a stroke laid him low, and the annual meeting on May 25, 1914, presided over by no less a figure than Prince Arthur of Connaught, was overshadowed by a sense of loss. Several months of rest brought no improvement, and he resigned the secretaryship of the Society in 1914. He was knighted in 1915, but was unable to receive the honour in person. He lingered on until January 1923, through the years of war and upheaval, a helpless spectator of changes so large and sudden that little of the old philosophy of the C.O.S. could survive. On his death, *The Times* (January 25, 1923) declared that ' "Loch of the C.O.S." was a household word among workers for the poor and public administrators'. 'He made the C.O.S.; he was the C.O.S.'

In a large sense this was true. He and the C.O.S. were a product of their time, of the last quarter of the nineteenth century, and much that they stood for could not survive into a different age. In another sense, fortunately, it was untrue. The C.O.S. survived. The part it played in the post-war world as a society was inevitably smaller; but in its principles of family casework and sound training for social work it found not only acceptance but a constantly wider influence.

[1] In the possession of Mrs R. B. Mowat.

Epilogue

The beginning of the First World War in 1914 plunged the C.O.S., like society as a whole, into an era of change, of which the end is not yet. British society has been passing through a great transformation, in which the two world wars of this century, the depression of the early 'thirties and the full employment of the years since 1945 have all played their part. Much greater equality exists in society than before: the old upper classes have relatively less wealth and leisure to spend upon charity and voluntary service; higher wages, better standards of housing and education, higher standards of living generally have brought about the disappearance of 'the poor', if not of people in poverty or need. In the inter-war years unemployment was a problem of such large, national proportions that it could not be left to the Guardians of the Poor; unemployment insurance and relief – a nationalised service of outdoor relief – relieved the Poor Law of much of its burden even before it was changed into Public Assistance.

Yet charity survived and there was plenty for it to do. Although the public social services were increasing, they were still far from complete, and many families and persons in need stood unsheltered, outside them. Voluntary hospitals, orphanages, convalescent homes, old peoples' homes, societies for the blind and the crippled continued to solicit funds and to carry on their work. New organisations were started, notably the National Council of Social Service (1919), whose very name indicated a new concern with needs that were not primarily material. Women's Institutes in the villages, and unemployed men's clubs in the distressed areas, were expressions of a new kind of social work. The C.O.S. was not idle. There were still families in trouble, whether from poverty or from some maladjustment; the social worker, more often a salaried caseworker than a volunteer, was still needed. The new housing estates of the London County Council and other local authorities provided a new field of work for the C.O.S.; modern houses in a new community which lacked the neighbourliness and the shops, public houses, churches, halls and cinemas of older towns, might become homes of quiet frustration without help from outside. The C.O.S. continued also to inquire into the larger social problems of the day: it took part, for example, in the movements for legislation on hire purchase and the adoption of children. On the outbreak of the Second World War it was still operating 30 District Offices. Its secretaries at the Central Office, after Loch, were the Rev. J. C. Pringle, 1914-19 and 1925-36, H. L. Woollcombe, 1919-23, M. W. Fox-Strangways, 1923-25 (acting secretary), and B. E. Astbury, 1936-56.

In the Second World War the C.O.S. was in the forefront of the agencies, public and voluntary, which ministered to the needs of victims of the blitz and of other wartime losses and bereavements. With the London Council of Social Service it promoted the Citizen's Advice Bureaux, and had 80 offices ready for operation when the war began. It had also laid in large stocks of blankets, clothes and food, thanks partly to the generosity of the Canadian Red Cross and other societies, and was able to give help of this sort – when food, clothes and sympathy were needed much more than money – before the authorities were ready to do so.[1]

---

[1] B. E. Astbury, 'Twenty-five years in the Family Welfare Association', *Social Work*, January 1956, is a valuable and warm-hearted retrospect.

Epilogue

After the war the Welfare State: universal and comprehensive where before the social services had been partial and incomplete. In the new equalitarian, high-employment society there might seem little place for the C.O.S. And the C.O.S. did change its name and its scale of work. In 1946 it became the Family Welfare Association. In 1949 it adopted a scheme of reorganisation: the District Committees (24 in 1945) were grouped into 10 areas, each with an Area Committee and an office; by 1956 the number of offices was 7. Family casework remains the staple of the Area Offices, but new functions have been assumed by the Association: in marriage guidance, help for old people, the giving of legal advice, aid to the families of coloured immigrants in settling themselves in strange and sometimes hostile surroundings. In 1958 the Association shared responsibility for 14 Citizens' Advice Bureaux and 2 Legal Advice Centres.

The F.W.A.'s *Annual Report* for 1958-59, proudly called the 90th and thus preserving continuity with the great series of C.O.S. *Annual Reports*, testifies to the Society's present vigour. There is a familiar air about it, for in the old tradition it contains case histories. The problems are no longer problems of poverty; some of them arise from strained financial resources, but most are not material at all: legal rights, broken homes, separations and divorces, mental stress are at the root of them. Important work is being done by the Old People's Home Committee in finding rooms, usually in private homes or voluntary old people's homes, for persons (not necessarily 'poor') who can no longer live alone. The F.W.A. administers 11 pension charities and disbursed £6,885 in 1958. The old Inquiry department is now the Information department: in 1956 it dealt with 2,509 inquiries, some relating to begging letter writers, most to the *bona fides* of charitable organisations from which persons had received appeals. The Area Committees – still the heart of

The Charity Organisation Society

the F.W.A.'s work – dealt with 2,912 new cases in 1958. The Association still publishes the *Annual Charities Register and Digest*. *How to Help Cases of Distress* now appears, since its 43rd edition (1950), as the *Guide to the Social Services*. The *Charity Organisation Review* became a quarterly in 1922, was renamed *Social Work* in 1939 and still appears each quarter. The Association's accounts show how its work is financed in these days. Much of its income comes from interest on investments – its own endowment – and from trust funds which it administers; much from City companies and business firms, from the City Parochial Foundation, the Carnegie United Kingdom Trust and other charities; a good deal from public authorities for special services. Even so, individual subscribers and donors number a thousand as proof that the older kind of charitable giving has not ceased.

These latter years have been years of encouragement as well as anxiety. There has been a great increase in attention to training for social work. In 1945, 17 British universities offered courses in preparation for social work; by 1951 the number was 22. Professional associations and local authorities also gave training. In London the F.W.A. had a large share in providing the practical work which all training programmes demand: in 1958 it gave training to 147 students, of whom 94 came from university social science departments. Both the scope and methods of courses for social workers were improved by the use made of American experience. In the United States social work had greatly developed during the inter-war years, while it had lain fallow in Great Britain; after the war knowledge of American practice and American methods of training began to flow back across the Atlantic.

As the profession of social work grew the opportunities for careers in it increased. Many social workers were specialists: hospital almoners, child care workers, probation officers, workers among the mentally deficient, and those engaged in

· 176 ·

group work and youth clubs. These were mostly employed by the local authorities and other public bodies; the general, family caseworkers had a rôle less clearly defined, if no less important in society, and were mostly working for a voluntary association, such as the F.W.A. or a local council of social service. They had formed their own professional organisation, the Association of General and Family Case-Workers.

In 1959 the professional status of the social worker was recognised by the publication of the Younghusband Report on *Social Workers in the Local Authority Health and Welfare Services*.[1] This paid tribute to the continuing work and vitality of the voluntary societies and the voluntary worker. Its demands for recognition of social work as a career, for greatly increased recruitment and training of 'general purpose social workers' and for better salaries and conditions, might gladden the hearts of the pioneers of the C.O.S. But these same pioneers, could they look upon our present society, would hardly approve of the domineering rôle of the public authorities in social work and the declining importance of charitable societies and personal, unpaid social work. Moreover, the more the status and rewards of social workers in the public services increase, the harder it will be for the voluntary societies to retain an efficient paid staff and to maintain their present position. From the public neglect of 'the poor' (except for the Poor Law) to public responsibility for social work – the wheel will have come full circle. But as long as social work is done in the manner of the C.O.S., by casework, and in the spirit of the C.O.S., concern for the individual and the family, the Welfare State will be drawing on the legacy of the Victorians who made the C.O.S. and devoted themselves to its work nearly a century ago.

[1] Ministry of Health, *Report of the Working Party on Social Workers in the Local Authority Health and Welfare Services*: Eileen L. Younghusband, chairman (H.M.S.O., 1959).

Bibliographical Note

The C.O.S. was always very active in publishing. My main source of information has been the *Annual Reports* of the Council, beginning with the first in 1870. These Reports were presented some time in the following year, in the spring or later, and it is not always clear to which year some passages relate: I have cited each Report by its number and the year it refers to, not the year in which it was presented. The District Committees published their annual reports separately. These are to be found, bound together for each year, in the C.O.S. library, but they were not usually distributed with the Council's *Annual Report*. *The Reporter* (weekly) was published from 1872 to 1884; it was succeeded from 1885 by the *Charity Organisation Review* (monthly), published in two series, 1885-96 and 1896 onwards. The *Annual Charities Register and Digest* began in 1882; the introduction, *How to Help Cases of Distress*, was first published separately in 1883. The many pamphlets, reprints of speeches, letters to *The Times*, and other material published by the Society were listed at the back of the *Annual Reports* and other publications. Several of these were numbered in a series, 'Charity Organisation Papers', Nos. 1-20, and published as *Charity Organisation Papers* in 1881 (enlarged in 1896 and reprinted in 1900 and 1907). A new series, 'Occasional Papers', also numbered, was published as *C.O.S. Occasional Papers* in four series, 1896, 1900, 1905, 1913 (the 1st series was also reprinted in 1907). The *Charity Organisation Series* was a series of books by different authors, edited by C. S. Loch and published by Swan Sonnenschein & Co.

Bibliographical Note

The Special Reports of the C.O.S. were in most cases published separately; the following list is probably not complete.

Conference on Night Refuges, 1870

Out-Patient Hospital Administration in the Metropolis, 1871

Report on the Metropolitan Charities Known as Soup-Kitchens and Dinner-Tables, 1871 (also *Soup Kitchens*, 1877)

The Crèches and Public Day Nurseries of London, 1872

Dwellings of the Poor, 1873 (another report on the same subject in 1881)

Training of the Blind, 1876

Education and Care of Idiots, Imbeciles and Harmless Lunatics, 1877

Italian Children, 1877

Convalescent Institutions, 1880

The Best Way of Dealing with Exceptional Distress, 1886 (also *The State and the Unemployed*, 1892)

Charity and Food 1887 (cf. *The Better Way of Assisting School Children*, 1893)

Audit of Accounts of Charitable Institutions, 1888 (also *Preparation and Audit of the Accounts of Charitable Institutions*, 1890)

Memorandum on Medical Charities of the Metropolis, 1889 (also *Survey of Metropolitan Medical Charities*, 1898)

Homeless Poor of London, 1891

Insurance and Saving, 1892

The Feeble-Minded Child and Adult, 1893

The Epileptic and Crippled Child and Adult, 1893
(These two volumes were in the Charity Organisation Series)

Relief of Distress due to Want of Employment, 1904

Unskilled Labour, 1908

The Charity Organisation Society

The writings of C. S. Loch appeared (often anonymously) in the *Charity Organisation Review*, in pamphlets published by the Society, in contributions to journals and to collections of papers (e.g. *Aspects of the Social Problem*, ed. B. Bosanquet, 1895, and *Old-Age Pensions*, 1903), and in the Annual Reports of the Society. His chief longer works were:

Charity Organisation, 1890

Methods of Social Advance (editor), 1904

Charity and Social Life, 1910

> This is a reprint of his article on Charity and Charities, published in 1902 in the supplementary volumes of the *Encyclopaedia Britannica* and most accessible in the 11th edition, 1910

A Great Ideal and its Champion: Papers and Addresses by the late Sir Charles Stewart Loch, 1923

Many of Loch's letters, and a diary which he kept from 1876 to 1888, and his commonplace books and sketch-books, are in possession of Mrs R. B. Mowat. For the most part they concern his private life and his family, and do not add much information about his public career and the ideas which he expressed in print.

Among secondary works the following are useful for the C.O.S. and its environment: Helen Bosanquet, *Social Work in London, 1869 to 1912: A History of the Charity Organisation Society* (1914); Karl de Schweinitz, *England's Road to Social Security* (Philadelphia, 1943); A. F. Young and E. T. Ashton, *British Social Work in the Nineteenth Century* (1956); Gertrude Williams, *The State and the Standard of Living* (1936); Helen M. Lynd, *England in the Eighteen-Eighties* (1945); Charles W. Pipkin, *Social Politics and Modern Democracies* (New York, 1931); B. Kirkman Grey, *Philanthropy and the State* (1908); A. F. C. Bourdillon, *Voluntary Social Services* (1945), especially Una Cormack's chapter, 'Developments in Case-Work'; Lord Beveridge, *Voluntary Action* (1948). Critical

Bibliographical Note

appraisals will be found in Sidney and Beatrice Webb, *English Poor Law History*, part II, vol. i (1929: in their 'History of English Local Government'); Beatrice Webb, *My Apprenticeship* (1926); Henrietta O. Barnett, *Canon Barnett, His Life, Work and Friends* (2 vols., 1919). The best life of Octavia Hill is by E. Moberly Bell (1942), and her ideas on charity will be found most readily in her essays, *Our Common Land* (1877).

Index

Index

Committee, 45, 46, 83, 84, 104; Council, meetings and work, 44-45, 87-88, 103-04, 169; Sub-Committees : convalescent homes, 86, 87, 88-89, 97; emigration, 89-90; inquiries, 46, 48; medical, 46, 88-89, 146; provincial, 93, 146, 150; thrift, 146; Central Office, work of, 47ff., 99; central finances, 47, 86-87, 145; assistant secretaries, 18, 20, 41, 85-86, 102, 145; Central Office staff, 86, 87, 145-6; inquiries section, 47-48, 175; library, 48-49; full title of C.O.S., 17, 50, 168-69, 170; special reports, 50ff.: night refuges, 50-52, 74; unemployment relief, (1871), 52, (1886), 131-134, (1904), 156; vagrancy, 52; street-sellers, 53; soup kitchens, 53, 74; Italian beggar-children, 53; day nurseries, 54; Octavia Hill's housing, 54; housing, 55-58; handicapped persons, 58, 75-76; idiots and mental defectives, 59, 76; medical charities, hospitals, 60-61, 79; voting charities, 61-62; school meals, 75; auditing of societies' accounts, 79; training, 108-12; lectures, 105-106, 111; unskilled labour, 157-158; relations with C.O. Societies in provinces, 44, 91-93, 106, 108, 146; co-operation with other charities, 21-23, 62, 88, 90, 150, 153-54; relations with charity organisation movement overseas, 93-95; C.O.S. conferences, 93, 95, 110, 146, 150, 172; C.O.S. pensions, 97-101, 145, 159,

175; beginning of salaried District Officers, 101ff.; District Secretaries, 83, 101-05, 147, 169; training of social workers, 105, 107-13, 170; public lectures on social work, 105-06; criticism of C.O.S., 126-30, 167, 168; views on old age pensions, 140-44; registration scheme, 151-53; R.C. on Poor Laws, 161-64; C.O.S. self-study, 1909, 168-69; history after 1913, 174; becomes Family Welfare Association, 175

Chicago School of Civics and Philanthropy, 110
Children's Country Holiday Fund, 45
Clay, Sir Arthur, 147, 156
Cowper-Temple, W., 19, 20
Cox, Frederick, 48, 51
Crowder, A. G., 115, 133, 168

D

Davison, H., 104
Davy, J. S., 116
Day nurseries, 54
Deaf and dumb children, 60
Denison, Edward, 11
Denison Club, 147-48
Denison House, 112, 147, 172
Derby, Earl of, 19, 20
Devon, Earl of, 59
Disenfranchisement of paupers, 59, 117, 134, 158, 160, 164
Dispensaries, 60-61
District Committee Aid Fund, 41, 47, 86, 87, 97, 145
District Committees of C.O.S.: Beginnings of, 21ff., 40, 146-47; co-operation with Poor Law, 22-24; work of District Offices,

Index

Index

Index

Index

W

Walrond, the Rev. M. S. A., 19, 133

Ward, Austin, 145

Waterlow, Sir Sidney, 55

Webb, Beatrice, 1, 118, 130-31, 160, 162-63

Wedgwood, A., 109

Westminster, Marquess of, 19, 20, 47, 50

Whitechapel Poor Law Union, 116, 117, 127, 132, 156

Wilkinson, W. M., 16, 17, 19, 52

Willink, H. G., 82, 115, 156

Women's University Settlement, 105-06

Woollcombe, H. L., 104, 109, 147, 174

Wright, J. Hornsby, 19

Wright, R. G., 145

Y

Yates, S. A. Thompson, 78

Younghusband Report on Social Workers, 1959, 177